Take an amazing woman boxer.
*Add an abandoned child growing up like
an animal on the beaches of California—
a deaf and mute child so troubled
that one social worker's report labeled
him "human garbage." Complicate the
story by incurring the wrath of organized
crime.*

*The result: The most unforgettable
true-life drama you have ever read.*

WILD CHILD

BY MARI HANES

LIVING BOOKS

Tyndale House Publishers, Inc.
Wheaton, Illinois

All Scripture references are taken from
the *King James Version* of the Bible (KJV)

Second printing, November 1982
Library of Congress Catalog Number 81-86694
ISBN 0-8423-8224-0

CONTENTS

A recent reunion with Mom Hall, the dorm mother at Teen Challenge in Los Angeles

FOREWORD

In the 1960s, I served as the director of the
Teen Challenge Addicts Choir in Los Angeles,
California. Those were powerful days in my life
—the choir I took on tour was probably the
most remarkable group of singers that ever got
together. Exaddicts, expushers, former prostitutes, and all kinds of former criminals came
together to sing about Jesus, the one who had
changed their lives and set them free.

Many heartbreaking cases came through the
doors of Teen Challenge. We worked with the
toughest of tough kids, but *no one* needed help
more desperately than Sandy!

My sister, Sandra, and I, as well as many
others, tried, really tried, to reach Sandy. His
situation seemed hopeless—with all of the
physical and emotional handicaps and drug
abuse. When Sandy left Teen Challenge, we lost
all contact with him, and I always thought, *The*

poor, tormented kid must have died from an overdose on one of those California beaches where he used to sit for hours.

Several years ago my group, the "Disciples," and I were on tour in the Northwest. A slender, Indian-looking boy with long hair and a huge grin slipped backstage and stood in front of me. It was Sandy—but a Sandy so changed that I could hardly believe it. As I reached out to grab his extended hand, I wondered, *Who in the world was able to get through to this wild child?* Standing behind him was a tall, motherly woman I later came to know as Naomi Tanner.

The story of Sandy and Naomi is even more dramatic than I could have guessed. A story like this can help a great many people for it will give them renewed hope. The Lord has no failures!

In His Love,
Andraé Crouch

INTRODUCTION

What would you do if you took into your home
a child who would only shower or bathe with
all of his clothes on? A child who refused to eat
at a table and devoured his food like a wolf cub.
A child who could not sleep in a bed since he'd
never had one and would not sleep except in a
blanket by the front door so he could "split" at
the first sign of trouble. What would you do
if this child were also deaf and used his own
brand of sign language to communicate, often
using vile gestures? How long could you stand it?

Sandy was that kind of child. When I first
heard Sandy's story and the story of Naomi
Tanner, the woman who took him into her
home, I could hardly believe a word of it. How
could a little boy have survived on his own
in the streets of Los Angeles from the time he
was barely five or six years old! And to think
that a situation like that could have existed in

America with its vast network of social services and organizations.

I took the time to do research on other "wild" children, children like Amala and Kamala captured in Midnapore, India, in 1920. They had been discovered living with a pack of wolves. Those two little girls, aged three and five, were mute, made occasional growling sounds, and walked on all fours. Throughout their next nine years in civilization, they persisted in eating raw meat.

Throughout history there have been many other cases such as that of a child nicknamed "Tarzancito." In December of 1933, he was captured in the jungles of El Salvador when he was approximately five years old. He had lived alone since a toddler, subsisting on a diet of wild fruit and raw fish. Newspaper correspondent Ernie Pyle, who had met Tarzancito, reported that when the boy first returned to human society, he communicated by howling and frequently attacked and bit people. Eventually Tarzancito learned to talk and adjusted to normal human life.

Later I met the "wild child," now a young man named Sandy Tanner. I found him *clothed and in his right mind.*

With sincere simplicity he began to convey to me his incredible story. We struggled to fit together the missing pieces and eventually were able to substantiate his bizarre memories with actual police records and institutional reports. Though last names and locations have been changed to protect Sandy and his adopted

family, this is *not* a book of fiction; it is a true-to-the-facts biography. It conveys, more than any other I have ever read or heard about, the overwhelming sense that
    no child is untouchable,
    no soul is unreachable,
    no situation is impossible.

                        Mari Hanes
                        1982

PART ONE

SANDY
Wilder than Wild

CHAPTER ONE

The policeman drew out his notebook to record the details of the complaint. "Lady, you'll have to calm down and give me a little more information," he said to the frantic woman opposite him. "First, let's start with a description of the juvenile delinquent who stole your purse."

"Officer, this was *not* a juvenile delinquent!" the woman exclaimed. "This was a *baby delinquent!*"

Even for a five-year-old, Sandy was little. Hereditary smallness and the lack of good care had made him a head shorter than other children his age. Fragile bones were laced together with a thin covering of olive skin. Street life didn't allow the soft, plump roundness common to a child his age.

His hair was long and black and thickly matted. His large solemn eyes were browner than brown. Any artist who saw him would've thought him a perfect model for one of the famous sketches of orphaned foreign waifs in tattered clothing.

The familiar sketches of street urchins with sad, saucerlike eyes often show children who look weak and listless. Sandy, however, was the opposite. He was as quick as a young animal. He darted, raced, and flew up one alley and down the next. He was almost impossible to catch.

Two facts enabled the lone five-year-old to survive. One was the Southern California climate. Although nights could grow cool, it was possible to live outside year round without freezing to death. Secondly, the little boy was extremely intelligent. However, his intelligence expressed itself in unusual ways. With little human influence, Sandy grew more and more savage. He developed special abilities common to the animal kingdom: instinct and cunning. He could reach out and grab something as quickly as a cat. He could scurry up walls and fences like a little monkey. He could flatten himself out to squeeze through even the slightest opening of a door or a window.

His favorite maneuver of all was the same one used by rabbits to elude a fox or coyote. Sandy had learned to run straight ahead, allowing his pursuer to grow tired and winded. Then, just when the enemy of the moment would put on one last burst of speed and reach out to grab him, Sandy would dart to the side and rush back past his startled adversary. This usually gave

Sandy such an edge that the exhausted pursuer would give up the chase.

A lone adult was no match for this boy. An angry storekeeper who had been "ripped-off" or a patrolman responding to an "abandoned child" report was totally frustrated if he tried to capture Sandy without reinforcements.

Many other children ran the streets, but Sandy was by far the youngest. His real source of danger was from the junior high gangs that roamed the city. (After years of coming into contact with dopers, gangsters, and hardened criminals of every kind, Sandy would later come to feel that some of those junior high boys were the meanest people he has ever known.)

A junior high boy was sometimes quick enough to catch Sandy, knocking him down to steal food in his possession or slugging him just for sport. So besides learning to run like an animal, Sandy quickly learned to hide like one. He could curl up in a tiny space and remain there for hours. He could hold his breath and control every muscle. His sense of hearing grew so sensitive that no one could approach him by surprise.

For months Sandy was on the move so much that he somehow escaped the attention of the authorities. Finally, though, there were so many reports of a "baby delinquent" that he became the object of an all-out search.

He can't remember the first time he was loaded, scratching and kicking, into the backseat of a police car. He remembers *many* times. The cunning animal-boy was good not only at avoiding capture but also at escaping. Once, he even bounded away just before being led through the front doors of the courthouse.

Each time he was picked up, the information which officials recorded was somewhat different. Los Angeles juvenile authorities did their best to piece together a history of the child for their files. The following report is typical:

NAME: Sandy (will give no last name)
AGE: probably 6 years old
DATE OF BIRTH: approximately 1960
RACE: Indian or Mexican
DATE OF JUVENILE'S APPREHENSION:
  May 30, 1966
COLOR OF EYES: Brown   **HAIR:** Black
SCHOOL: None   **GRADE:** None
CHARGES: several minor thefts, mostly pocket
              money and food; accused of
              breaking and entering vacant
              buildings; accused of biting and
              kicking a salesclerk; most reports
              deal with the child's loitering; is
              apparently abandoned
PERSON(S) FILING COMPLAINT: Mrs. C.
  Walker, Mr. Richard Kenfield, Mr. Donald
  O'Shane
PARENTS' NAMES AND ADDRESS: appar-
  ently unknown
PARENTS NOTIFIED: Search for any relatives
  has proven futile
COMMENTS: This is the child who has been
              reported in various sections of
              the city. He is extremely unco-

operative, violent, and destructive. He remains crouched in the corner like a little wild man, kicking and spitting on anyone who comes near him. He at first appears to be American Indian, but what little he says shows a Southern drawl; he could be the child of migrant workers from the deep South or even of Mexican descent. Obvious emotional illness. *Probably mental retardation.*

ARRESTING OFFICER: Darrell Noble
RELEASED TO: County Children's Holding Center—Montrose Ward #32. Solitary confinement suggested until medical evaluation is complete.

Eventually, Sandy found it easier to make up last names than say he was "Sandy No-name." Sometimes he was Sandy Ortiz or Sandy Jones or Sandy Cruz. It is virtually impossible to trace down all of the juvenile files opened under Sandy's name. In all, files were opened under at least twenty different surnames. The most amazing fact of all is that sometimes Sandy was listed as male; sometimes as female.

After being taken to the police station, six-year-old Sandy would be sent to a child-processing center like the one in Montrose. Although not meant to be, these centers were often a troubled child's first experience with "jail." Delinquents under twelve years of age were placed in the centers on charges ranging from arson to armed assault. Other children at those centers had committed no crimes: their parents had been sent to prison, leaving them homeless.

The doors were locked; the windows were barred. The halls were drab and gloomy. There were stern matrons with harsh voices. And among the children, there evolved a hierarchy of power exactly like that found among adult prison inmates. Anyone visiting a center for the first time had the eerie feeling he had walked into a scene from an old Charles Dickens' story— perhaps into a debtor's prison filled with street urchins.

More often, Sandy was taken immediately from a police station to a hospital, such as Metropolitan General, the massive brick fortress in Santa Ana.

"Colleen, there's a little kid in Room 507 that I want you to handle," the doctor told his nurse. "Better take a couple of interns with you."

"How old is the child?"

"Seven or eight."

"Seven or eight, and I'll need a couple of interns!"

"You'll need at *least* two assistants," the physician stated firmly. "This boy was in here a couple of months ago, and he's a real wild cat. Just try to get him out of his filthy street clothes and into a hospital gown."

"What tests should I schedule him for?"

Colleen knew her duties well. "Routine physical exam and mental competency tests?"

"No. This afternoon we'll try to sedate him and prep him for surgery. The last examination showed the urgent need for it. We aren't sure if the cause was birth defects or street injuries, but there are real problems in the male organs. We need to construct a new urinary tract. Then, if we can keep up with the little hellion, in a couple of years we'll need to operate again, or he will never develop normally."

Colleen was no newcomer to the Children's Mental Health Ward. In ten years the stout nurse had seen almost everything, and her muscles had been toughened by many an angry, fighting child. Still, she took the doctor's advice. Two strong young interns followed her into Room 507. *If only my heart could be toughened up like my muscles,* she thought.

But there wasn't much room for sympathy when she entered the room. The child crouching in a corner of the room was like the wildcat the surgeon had described. The boy's skin, his hair, and his stinking garments were covered with grey film—street dirt. In an instant Colleen saw that his snarling teeth and long, dirty fingernails would be vicious weapons. She could glimpse only a little of his face; he was wearing a huge, battered, black cowboy hat.

The fight that followed went the full twelve rounds. Screams, grunts, and curse words filled the air. The nurse and the two interns were determined, but at times the small child actually seemed to be winning. For one thing, the adults had to remove seven complete layers of clothing from his struggling body. Finally the nurse pinned arms and head. "We'll have to delouse his hair after he's sedated!" she shouted. One intern pinned Sandy's legs, and the other was able to get him into the hospital gown.

When the struggle was over, the wildcat sat panting on the bed. "Thanks, guys," Colleen said and smiled their dismissal. "I'll call you later if we need you."

The veteran nurse, turning to follow the men from the room, rubbed a bruised arm and knew her face had been badly scratched. Her eyes fell upon the tattered black hat on the floor, and she picked it up to carry it with her to the burning bins.

In one jump, Sandy leaped off the bed and tackled the woman around the knees. With a loud yell, the surprised nurse crashed to the floor. By the time the doctor raced into the room, Sandy was back on the bed, the cowboy hat pulled down over his glaring eyes.

"The little animal *tackled* me!" the nurse sputtered as she was helped to her feet. "He *tackled me!*" Losing all self-control, she turned to pounce on the boy.

But the child was grinning from ear to ear.

Somehow his disarming smile pulled a smile from the doctor, then a laugh. Suddenly, the tough, old nurse caught the humor of the situation . . . and *she* began laughing.

And Sandy got to keep his hat.

CHAPTER TWO

Another boy of the streets had given Sandy the old, black cowboy hat. Pitiful and worn as it was, it was the only "present" the little boy had ever received. Everything else—from food to his layers of crusty clothing—had been stolen. The tattered hat was his only treasure—he would have died for that dusty bit of felt.

Even in the long run, the black hat proved tremendously valuable to Sandy. It is one of his few concrete memories, and one of the "trade-marks" people remembered years later which enabled a young man without a history to piece together some of the fragments of his past.

Countless children have passed through Metropolitan General Hospital. The doctors and nurses on the staff remember only a few. Shown Sandy's current picture, they only shrug and say, "I'm not sure I remember." However, *many* remember a wild animal-boy dressed in a white hospital gown and a ridiculous cowboy hat on his way to different examination areas.

The records show that Sandy remained at the hospital long enough to have corrective surgery done on the male organs. It was to be only the initial treatment, but as his doctor had feared, Sandy "split" before he received further treatment, running from the medical help he so desperately needed.

Sandy returned to the peril of the streets.

The next few years are totally blank in his memory. Somehow he continued to survive, leaving a hellish childhood behind and moving into an even more hellish adolescence. Sandy had no concept of the passage of weeks or months or seasons. He marked the passage of time only according to the Christmas decorations which were hung each December in city streets. When asked how much longer he stayed on the streets of Los Angeles, he now simply says, "About three Christmases."

Often, our minds subconsciously cover painful memories. There is an even easier explanation for Sandy's lack of recall. He was a child alcoholic. Booze made him warm and happy. It was filling and as easy to steal as food. His thirst was unquenchable by the time he was eleven years old.

People who hear Sandy's story today are amazed that as a child, he could not have been somehow tracked down, confined, and helped. It probably would have been possible except for the era of American history with which his life coincided: the sixties, the decade of the hippy movement.

Well-educated, well-to-do teenagers from all across America were flooding the streets of California. Disillusioned and searching, these "flower children" talked of love and peace, discarded conventional dress and hairstyles, and turned on to psychedelic drugs.

In the masses of the hippy movement, Sandy could easily melt into the crowd. He became untraceable. His long, matted hair and disheveled clothing were in perfect style.

For the first time in years, Sandy didn't always live alone. He remembers being welcomed into communal tenement buildings, spending nights in an apartment with fifteen to twenty other young people. They required nothing of him, no history, no last name. They often shared food with him and were always willing to share their drugs. He never left booze behind, but added to it every kind of pill.

He started with LSD—"acid." One night a boy, not much older than Sandy, sat blowing into a toy harmonica and offered him a pill. "Take this, kid. It will open your mind and like wow, you'll be able to *see* the music."

Sandy took one and then two of the pills. If one helped him see music, what would two do? The boy gave him the harmonica and left. Sandy never saw music. He saw a lot of other things instead: monsters, hideous demons, the thunder and the lightning of childhood terror. It was the beginning of hundreds of "bad trips," of grotesque nightmares from which he could never escape.

Instead of remaining in the Los Angeles area, Sandy began to move up and down the California coastline, following the sporadic migrations of his hippy acquaintances. For several months, he lived in San Francisco in the now famous Haight-Ashbury District. Some nights still found him sleeping outside. When cold weather hit, the Bay area fog drove him back to the warmer climate of Los Angeles.

One of the hardest facts to comprehend about Sandy's existence was that he had almost no understanding of sexuality. He knew there was a difference between men and women; mainly he conceived it as a difference in size and strength. He also knew that "mommas" could eventually nurse a baby. He watched men and women lie together in the communal rooms where he often stayed. He had seen dogs and other animals mating. He learned to jive and joke at that, along with his companions.

Yet as a young teenager, his own sexual drive was lacking. His treatment at Metropolitan General had never been completed, and he was not maturing as he should. There were also severe hormonal complications.

Sandy had no physical relationships. He hated to be touched. And why not? He had never experienced love or affection.

Had anyone sexually molested him or bothered him in those days? He doesn't think so. Later he would live through the terror of sexual abuse, the degradation of being "used." But in the communal setting, Sandy's abuse came at the hand of the demons behind "uppers" and "downers."

After a few years, the love and peace the flower children sought became more elusive than ever. The ills of society that the flower children sought to escape worked their way into the communal lifestyle, though on a somewhat smaller scale. Greed, jealousy, and anger are not so easily removed from the human character. Sometimes without knowing what he had done, he would incur the wrath of one of the "family members." Sometimes the reason was more clear to him: he had taken too much food, too many drugs, or maybe had "looked at somebody the wrong way."

Once he angered the muscular black leader of one of the houses by lying down beside that man's girl friend. Sandy was drunk, exhausted, and had meant no harm. He was beaten unmercifully. Blood ran from his ears for three days.

Eventually Sandy was sick of the run-ins and simply began to be on "his own" again. He found a fantastic home—a huge culvert pipe leading into the concrete bed of the Los Angeles River. The river was dry most of the year. The eight-foot-high drain pipe was a snug shelter, good for storage and almost private except for the occasional bums who shared his dwelling. Sandy didn't mind them—they were slow and harmless. He often gave them food.

The boy never thought in terms of whether or not he was happy. Happiness was an unknown concept. He thought in terms of whether he was "full" or "hungry" and "well" or "hurting." He liked the culvert he had found to live in. He didn't realize that he was lonely.

Soon, however, the recognition of loneliness crept into his heart like a silent tiger, stalking him and preying on his soul. It came as sincere, concerned adults began to try to reach an unreachable child. Their well-meaning attempts at friendship helped release the tiger. That, more than the drugs or street life, almost destroyed him.

CHAPTER THREE

Sandy hated the blue vans. Whenever he had
passed out on the streets and been taken to
Metropolitan Hospital, he would try to escape
just as he had after his operation. If he didn't
get away in time, they would put him into
one of those blue vans. And the vans always
took him to a children's detention center.

But this time he was older. His record was
longer. The cops who picked him up placed him
in a van which took him in a different direction.
They meandered through the crunch of a rush-
hour traffic, got on an eastbound freeway, and
drove far away from Los Angeles into the rolling
California hills. Finally, the van turned in at the
gates of the Camarillo Institute for Juveniles.

Laura Landon, an attractive young counselor,
was in charge of the receiving desk the morning
Sandy was "hauled in."

"Get a 'TNT' shirt on him. And *keep* him in it

all the time!" Laura was adamant after having read Sandy's file from Metro General.

Sandy was proud of the "TNT" shirt with its big black letters on the white background. He couldn't read them, but they looked "cool." To the Camarillo staff, the "TNT" shirt meant several things: "explosive," "a child to be watched at all times," "possibly dangerous," and "will attempt to go AWOL."

As soon as Sandy was taken from Laura's office to the cafeteria for his first meal at Camarillo, Laura followed an impulse she usually considered highly unprofessional. She went to the director's office and begged to be the staff member who would oversee Sandy's treatment. Dr. Hal Enloe's reponse to her request was positive. Then as she sat at her desk, typing a "Treatment Procedures File" for her new charge, she thought how ironic the title seemed.

Camarillo was already too crowded with deeply disturbed young people to "treat" any of them effectively. The juveniles ranged in age from twelve to eighteen years old. All had criminal records. Some were thieves. Others had committed armed assaults; a few were even murderers.

Basically, we'll just be like a holding tank for this poor kid, Laura reminded herself. *We can feed him three meals a day—which he desperately needs—and we can keep him off the drugs and booze.* "And I can *test* him!" she told her typewriter, which often had to listen to Laura when no one was around. "I can test him so thoroughly that at least his file will show what his needs *really* are!"

Young and inexperienced, in her first position after graduating from UCLA, Laura *knew* dealing with this boy called Sandy would be a mountain of a job.

The evaluation committee met weekly at Camarillo, but it was two months before Laura was ready to face the committee with the file of a child who was "hardly even human."

For those entire two months, Laura felt as if she were holding her breath. Day after day, Laura attempted to gain the boy's trust, but Sandy rejected her attempts at friendship. Sandy could easily "freak out" and run away at any time. His sketchy reports showed that the longest he had been detained anywhere was two weeks.

At Camarillo, though, Laura had one thing in her favor and she wasn't aware of it. Camarillo had a big yellow school bus for taking the juveniles on occasional field trips.

The sight of that old bus parked inside the gates was like a security blanket for Sandy. Tucked away in his subconscious was the memory of an old yellow bus which had been home for a child who had traveled with migrant workers. For that reason alone, Camarillo gave Sandy a strange, wordless sort of contentment and kept him within the institution despite Laura's extensive testings. The high point of his life was the Friday morning excursions when he could bounce through the rolling California hills in the big yellow bus.

On May 15, 1970, the five-member evaluation committee met to consider the results of Laura's studies. The meeting lasted hours. At the end, the five social workers could not agree on a method of treatment. Only one thing was unanimous: Sandy's case was the most difficult and complicated they had ever seen.

Sandy had been given both the Stanford-Binet Intelligence Test and the Wechsler Intelligence Test for Children. His score, in the low sixties, labeled him "retarded." Though certain that Sandy was *not* retarded and that she had gained only his partial cooperation during the testing, Laura still had to report the facts as they were.

Sandy also received the Rorschach Personality Test—a series of ink blots to which he had to respond quickly and relate what he saw in the shapes. Finally, Laura gave him the Thematic Apperception Scale—a series of black and white pictures about which he had to make up stories. In every situation, Sandy's responses were bizarre and frightening.

The same morning during which Laura gave her extensive report to the evaluation committee, Sandy went on a field trip on the yellow bus. Sixteen teenagers traveled twenty miles to see a fish hatchery.

At the hatchery one of the bigger boys hassled Sandy, and the animal-boy flew into a rage. Forgetting about the yellow bus and the good meals he'd had at Camarillo, Sandy made an instant decision to "split." As he took off across an open field, his "TNT" shirt stood out like a beacon. And still he could not be caught.

The chairman of the evaluation committee had no choice but to close Sandy's file with the following report:

In view of the severe emotional instability, mental and social retardation, and violent disposition of this boy, this committee recommends that the next time the youth is apprehended he be confined in a maximum security mental institution.

Natural handicaps and environmental forces have produced a being more animal than human, an unreachable boy who could aptly be classified as *human garbage*.

Sandy has no legal guardian, and must remain a ward of the state to be retained in a mental hospital, scheduled for reevaluation only when reaching the approximate age of twenty-one.

Laura wept when she read the report. "Human garbage," they'd called him, but the recommendation was accurate. The boy was unreachable and beyond help. Next time he was arrested, he would be assigned to the nearest mental hospital.

The next day Laura resigned from the Camarillo staff and took a job as a florist near her home.

Within six months, Sandy was once again apprehended. This time there were no tests and no concerned social workers—nothing but an evaluation which included the phrase "classified as human garbage." As the report recommended, he was incarcerated at a mental institution—Western State near San Jose—and would be

scheduled for reevaluation only when he
reached the approximate age of twenty-one.

Sandy knew that Western State was a "crazy
farm." He didn't feel crazy. However, he did feel
angry—burningly, destructively angry. Seething
with humiliation, he lashed out at anyone who
came near him. An attendant could hardly
deliver a meal to his locked, windowless room
and escape without teeth marks and bruises.

Sandy was placed in a straight jacket. He was
drugged and even received electric shock
therapy. Yet none of those traumatic treatments
came even close to accomplishing the usual
passivity. During the first four weeks of being
institutionalized, Sandy spent his days the same
way—crouching in a corner of the recreation
room. There he snarled and hissed, seeming to
be more of an animal than he had ever come
close to being. He was not even allowed outside
within the fenced yards of Western State.

Finally he was released from solitary confinement. His violence made most of the overworked
staff steer clear of him. It could not, however,
save Sandy from sexual degradation at the hands
of the other inmates.

From even the gangs in Los Angeles, Sandy
had escaped rape and sexual abuse, but now the
slender, young teenager was confined with
criminally insane men of brutal strength. During
those long and hellish nights in the mental
wards, he was misused and forced into every
kind of sexual perversion.

Had the boy been mentally weak or even
retarded, he would have been totally broken by

this time. Somehow his angry spirit did *not* break. With amazing craftiness, his instincts soon pointed to a way of escape.

One morning Sandy noticed the large air-conditioning ducts in some of the hallways. The cover could be pried off one of those vents. The openings were small, but so was he. After all, hadn't he once escaped from Metropolitan General Hospital by sliding down a laundry chute?

That same night Sandy convinced one of the kindlier patients, an old man named Jethro, to boost him up so that he could reach the vent cover and swing up into the opening.

As Jethro hoisted Sandy to his shoulders, the boy's long hair swung into the old man's face.

"Hell, what a ton of hair!" Jethro exclaimed. "You could pass for a little momma for sure! If you really get out, kid, give it a try. The cops will all be looking for a runaway boy."

Sandy inched along the labyrinth of the air-conditioning system in the total blackness of night. Many times he became so wedged in the aluminum tunnel that he thought he would suffocate and die in the endless maze. Once he pushed so hard to turn a corner that he actually pulled his shoulder bone out of its socket. With indescribable agony, he popped it back into place and simply continued on. Sandy was tough—as tough and as determined as a human being could be.

Finally, just before dawn, he found his way into the staff quarters. It was 3:00 A.M. and the few overnight attendants had already sunk into deep sleep. Sandy dropped onto a hallway floor and climbed out through an unbarred window. He was *free.*

Like a wild Indian pony, he began loping across an open field. His shoulder exploded with pain at the jolt of each stride, but Sandy never stopped grinning. *Sandy will never be taken back to that "crazy farm." Sandy will knife himself bad and bleed and die before he comes near here ever anymore.*

One thing stuck in his mind as he ran that night: *Be a little momma.* Sound advice. Sandy knew it could be easily accomplished if he combed his hair a little and added a few layers of Saran Wrap in the right places. The all-points bulletin issued that night was for a missing teenaged *boy.* Sandy never *said* he was a girl, but he allowed all of the confusion with good reason. Thus began the sex-confusion that would last for seven years.

CHAPTER FOUR

. . . It was the Friday night before Christmas 1970. All of the women who lived at the Teen Challenge Girls Home had gone to the Teen Challenge Center for a Christmas party. Marion Sweitzer, dorm parent to the women, had remained behind to baby-sit the children of the female addicts.

At 9:00 A.M. the doorbell rang. Marion opened the door to a stranger in Levi's and a filthy jacket. It was Sandy. Swaying slightly, he raised an empty beer can in greeting and asked in a slurred voice, "Is party here?" Sandy had heard about the Christmas party from invitations passed out on the streets.

Marion shook her head. "No, the party's not here, but we have hot coffee and food. Come on in."

She managed to get Sandy into the kitchen, but before he was able to eat anything, he passed out on the floor. More than twenty-four hours later, he regained consciousness.

The first person he saw was a pretty, young woman who spoke kindly. "I'm Faith," she said simply. "We're going to help you."

Sandy gazed at her as if to ask, "Why bother?" He knew this was no police station, hospital, or state farm. Why would they want to take in a stranger?

"I was lost once, too, and killing myself with heroin, but not anymore," Faith continued gently. "These people are here to help girls like us who have no one else to turn to. They are here because Jesus loves everyone, including me and you."

"Love?" Sandy gruffed with an odd mixture of bitterness and indifference. "What that be?"

Thinking he was a girl, the women gave him a room in their dorm. Sandy left as soon as he was strong enough, but not before he had had a taste of the love and compassion which flowed as freely as the good food at the Center.

Two months later, Faith, Marion, and a counselor named Mom Hall were walking toward their car when suddenly Faith screamed. Face down in the driveway was a body. As they rolled the person over, they gasped. It was Sandy. His face was bloody and battered. His fists were clenched; one of them held a knife. "She's still breathing!" Marion said.

Inside, the women prayed for Sandy, had the nurse give first aid, and then took turns watching Sandy all night.

The next morning Sandy was conscious and

quiet. A few hours later, however, a destructive force suddenly seemed to seize the teenager. He was literally tearing up the room—furniture and all. It took four strong women to get him upstairs to the room for addicts undergoing withdrawals. Mattresses were placed on the floor to soften falls. The room held no furniture.

Many times during the next three days, Sandy sprang at the workers with the fury of an angry young tiger. He screamed, beat his head on the walls, and swore continually. Two workers watched over Sandy constantly until at last he seemed to return to reality—from the very grip of Satan.

Sandy stayed at the Center for five days, listening to the women sing, play their guitars, and read their Bibles. To that point he hadn't known what a Bible was. And of course, he ate whatever they offered him. He refused to sit at the long dining hall table, choosing instead to crouch in a corner and devour his meal like a starving, stray dog.

The women offered him clean new clothes. They, of course, thought he was the filthiest young girl who had ever walked through the Center's doors. Sandy never actually *told* them, "I'm a girl," but for one year, Sandy had been following the advice given to him the night he escaped the mental institution: "Act like a little momma." Sandy had let his hair grow and had "padded" himself in all the right places with plastic garbage sacks. Besides making himself look more like a female, Sandy discovered that the plastic wrappings provided great insulation.

Sandy firmly refused the new clothes. When one of the women went so far as to offer Sandy a new brassiere, he literally flew into a rage.

"Relax, honey!" the puzzled worker pleaded. "I never thought any girl would be so offended by a new bra!"

In spite of violent temper flare-ups and the trouble the workers had understanding Sandy's terribly garbled speech, the women felt they were getting somewhere. That's why they were dismayed one morning when Sandy simply disappeared.

One Friday night, a group of Christians were handing out tracts at Fifth and Main in downtown Los Angeles. Most of the passersby ignored them, but a boyish-looking teenaged "girl" stayed at the corner, watching them out of troubled eyes. It was Sandy. His shoulders were hunched forward. One arm was pressed to his side as if he were in intense pain.

A Christian girl named Lori watched Sandy, who felt ready for anything but a friendly chat. Lori handed Sandy a tract. After giving it an angry glance, Sandy threw it into the gutter. Lori handed him a new tract for each one Sandy threw down. Finally Lori invited Sandy to a nearby restaurant. "How about getting a Coke down the street?" she asked. Instantly Sandy turned to walk away, but compelled by hunger and by the kind look in Lori's eyes, he returned.

He followed her to a booth in the restaurant, and she ordered them both hamburgers.

"My name is Lori. What's yours?" Sandy was silent. "I'm only trying to find a way to talk to you because I think the Lord wants me to. He cares about us all. He cares that you're hurting tonight,'' Lori said softly.

At the mention of God, Sandy became engulfed with fury and drew his fist back to swing.

"You don't really want to hit me, do you?'' Lori asked. Something Sandy saw in the girl's eyes caused his hand to unclench and fall limp to his side. Sandy's other arm was still pressed against the tattered jacket.

"You've been stabbed, haven't you?'' Lori asked and gave Sandy a card on which were printed the Teen Challenge address and phone number. "Do you know about Teen Challenge? I've never been there,'' Lori said, "but I know that you'd be welcome. I'll take you there if you'd like.''

The mention of Teen Challenge flooded Sandy with memories of Marion, Faith, Mom Hall, and the others. Sandy's eyes lit up momentarily but then grew cloudy. He grabbed a handful of napkins and stuffed them under his blood-soaked coat. Then he stood, picked up the remainder of his burger, and walked away from the table without even a nod of thanks.

He moved quickly in spite of the intense pain.

Lori immediately telephoned the women's dorm of Teen Challenge only to discover that Marion and her co-workers had already provided food and shelter several times for the teenager she described. "We'll be watching for Sandy,'' Marion told Lori. "She has a special place in all of our hearts. And we will all be praying.''

During the night, Marion awoke several times

and prayed for Sandy. She knew it would make the difference. When she began reading her Bible at one point during the night, her eyes fell on the words from Jeremiah:

I will heal the wounds.

She claimed them for Sandy.

Sandy didn't show up at the Center the next day or during that week. A month passed. Early one morning, the dorm phone rang shrilly. Faith answered it.

"We've done that little bitch over good," a harsh female voice said. "If you want her, you'd better come and get her." The voice rambled on, punctuating every statement with vile profanity.

"What are you talking about?" Faith demanded.

The voice spewed forth a string of curses. "Don't tell me you don't know this Indian kid! The sucker has a Teen Challenge card in her pocket."

Faith's heart pounded as she remembered Lori's call and knew that the Indian kid they were talking about was Sandy. "Is—is she all right?"

The caller said calmly, "I think she's dead." The phone clicked.

Every one at the Center, including counselors and addicts, searched the streets for Sandy. They scoured alleys, playgrounds, and parks all day. Discouraged and weary, they returned to the Center that night.

To their surprise, who should be on the

doorsteps of the Center but Sandy! Had a gang dumped him there? Had he managed to crawl to the Center? No one knew and Sandy couldn't remember. Somehow, by God's mercy, Sandy was still alive.

Many times in the new year—1971—Sandy showed up to spend a few nights at the dormitory. Once when he arrived in a drugged stupor, Mom Hall and Marion removed his coat and found that Sandy had arrived with presents for all of his friends. He'd taped a multitude of small items to his shirt, including a sack of small toy chickens for Easter baskets. When Sandy became sober, he presented everyone he knew at the Center with the gift of an Easter chicken.

Another time Sandy limped through the doors with a badly broken foot. Through words and gestures, he conveyed that he had been chased through an abandoned tenement by two policemen and had escaped by jumping from a third-story window.

The broken foot took weeks to heal—weeks that kept Sandy confined to the Center. It was during this time that Sandy made friends with Andraé Crouch and his sister, Sandra.

Andraé was the choir director and pianist for the Teen Challenge Choir, comprised of expushers and exprostitutes. Traveling across the nation, they had made a powerful impact with their testimony of God's grace. In the years to come, Andraé would soar to worldwide fame and win Grammies for his singing and songwriting. Nevertheless, no audience would ever be more loving and appreciative than the broken young men and women at Teen Challenge.

Andraé and Sandy first met during a choir rehearsal in the Center's chapel. Sandy had not allowed a doctor to come near his broken foot. Even without a cast, it was somehow mending. Sandy was hurrying to the stage to be close to the good music when suddenly his injured foot gave way. He fell to his knees, then to the floor. Determined and strong-willed as ever, Sandy simply crawled the rest of the way to the piano which Andraé was playing.

Andraé looked directly into Sandy's eyes and began singing completely for him:

He touched me.
Yes, He touched me.
And oh, the joy that floods my soul!
Something happened, and now I know
God touched me and made me whole.

Sandy was deeply stirred. He loved music but had never been moved in this way. Impulsively he reached up and touched Andraé's face and then placed his own hand over his heart. Sandy seemed to be asking an urgent question, "Do you really believe in this God that you sing about?"

Andraé continued to sing:

Is there anyone who can help me,
One who understands my needs?
Is there anywhere I can go?
All my life I've wandered to and fro.
Won't somebody help me? Won't somebody help me,
  please?

Help me, for I'm in despair,
Can't believe that anybody cares,
For my life is abused and my mind is confused.
My heart is filled with fears,
And my eyes are filled with tears.
Won't somebody help me? Won't somebody help me,
*   please?*

When will I be free from this misery?
When will I find rest for this weary mind?
Won't somebody help me, for I'm lost. . . .

Sandy had tears in his eyes. Still sitting on the
floor, he couldn't keep his shoulders from
shaking with sobs. He covered his face with
trembling hands and then wept brokenheartedly
as he had never wept before.

CHAPTER FIVE

Moments after dawn, San Fernando Boulevard was almost deserted. Sandy stepped out into the crosswalk and limped across the street. His broken foot was mending, but the aching tenderness caused him to move slowly.

Suddenly, as if from nowhere, a red pickup truck raced past him and actually brushed against one of his sleeves. Sandy froze momentarily, then continued across the boulevard. Leaning against a lamp post, he closed his eyes and broke into a cold sweat. He'd stepped directly in front of the vehicle, and the driver had swerved barely in time to avoid catastrophe.

Sandy hadn't looked carefully, he knew, and it was obvious that the driver had been speeding. Still, in the past he had never come so close to getting "wiped out." His keen ears would've heard the car coming, but this time Sandy had heard absolutely nothing at all.

He realized he was going deaf. His hearing continued to come and go for some months. During that time Andraé Crouch became Sandy's special friend. Sometimes Sandy accompanied him to the recording studios where the choir cut records. At times Sandy could hear and would listen with such undivided attention that he seemed to be in a trance. He would pull a battered harmonica from his pocket and hold it on his lap so that the others in the studio could see that he too was a musician.

At other times Sandy seemed frustrated. He'd walk up to the piano and lay his head on the wood in an attempt to "hear." Often he couldn't hear a single note but simply felt the rhythmic vibrations of the strings.

At the Center, Sandy treasured the unpredictable moments he had in the world of sound and music. Some nights in his room, he could hear well enough to pick out bits and pieces of the songs Andraé had played on the piano. Sandy taught himself almost all of "He Touched Me."

When Sandy couldn't hear, he still liked to play his harmonica. If he blew hard enough, he could feel the vibrations in his lips and teeth.

Because his deafness came slowly like dark clouds gathering to hide the light of the sun, Sandy had enough time to learn to read lips. Not intentionally, but naturally, Sandy found he could understand what people were saying to him almost as well as if he could hear them.

His vocabulary had always been limited; his talking, somewhat slurred. Now his speech suffered even more because Sandy couldn't tell whether he was whispering or shouting. He had always used many gestures to communicate—most of them profane. Now he improvised new ways to talk with his hands.

Sandy would go to the Teen Challenge Center for a few nights of good food and sobriety and then be back on the streets for days of drugs and danger. He kept up the pattern—Center, streets, Center, streets. Sandy loved Teen Challenge, but he didn't stay there long enough to be really helped or changed.

Marion, Faith, Mom Hall, Andraé, Sandra, and the other workers continued to love and accept him. Sandy learned much later that though they had been outwardly very patient with him, inwardly, they had felt more and more discouraged. After all, their combined efforts hadn't made an impact on Sandy's life. Or so they thought.

SUMMER 1971

Shirley Stanton had left her home in Missouri and moved to California to attend a Bible college. She spent her spring and summer breaks at the Center doing volunteer counseling. Shirley had not come to Teen Challenge "off the streets" as had most of the other workers, but still she was well respected and well loved. There was something so profound, so vibrant about her spirit, that she found instant rapport with even the toughest young hoodlums.

Shirley's heart broke when she met Sandy.

"Don't get involved with that kid," the others warned her. "We've all tried to help her. There's nothing more that you could possibly do."

But Shirley got involved. Throughout the hot, smoggy Los Angeles summer, she befriended Sandy whenever he showed up at the Center. She took walks with him and sat with him at mealtimes. Better than anyone else, she learned to understand Sandy's special kind of sign language. Shirley even offered him a home. "I'm getting married soon to a wonderful man named John," she told Sandy often. One evening she took him aside and said, "After John and I are married, we want you to come and live with us. Forever. You would be like our daughter. We would be a real family."

A family? Does Shirley mean a family like those smiley-faced people sitting around a dinner table? The ones I saw when I looked in their windows from outside at night? Sandy wondered. *A real family?*

Sandy couldn't answer. His lips couldn't move. His arms felt too weak to attempt to make signs. It was hard for him to believe that anyone could actually care enough for him to invite him to live in a *real house* and to stay *forever.*

Shirley and her fiancé, John Braddock, had talked about that idea for some time. They had also prayerfully considered adopting Sandy as their "daughter," feeling it was God's will that they open their home to this child of the streets.

Shirley repeated her offer of a home every few days. By the time the wedding date arrived, Sandy realized that his friends actually *meant* it. After the wedding, John and Shirley moved to

Missouri to begin a ministry there. Sandy packed his harmonica and his few other treasures in a paper bag and went with them.

A big change came over Sandy in Missouri. He smiled often and seemed to have genuine affection for the Braddocks. He—or "she" as they thought—still would let no one near when he changed clothes. He even refused to be taken to a doctor to have a hearing examination. "But that will come in time," Shirley and John encouraged each other.

Making use of expressive pantomime, Sandy dictated a letter to Marion and the others at Teen Challenge shortly after his arrival in Missouri:

Dear Nana, [The young people at the Center often called Marion "Nana."]

When we left the big house, we came a long way down here to Shirley and John's house. It is fine with lots of trees. We unpacked Shirley's things. The car had lots of boxes on top of it and in the trunk were boxes. I have never seen so many, many things before.

Shirley laughs a whole bunch and talks about everything and jumps up and down. Sandy sees Shirley get happy and gets happy, too. There are lots of chickens and tame rabbits and some birds in the yard John calls "peacocks."

There is one duck and he isn't white—he's ugly. That's OK, though. I like him a little bit.

Sandy is happy more than in a long, long time. Sandy thinks that this is all dreaming.

At the bottom of the page, in sweeping and uncertain letters that Shirley was teaching him, Sandy signed his own name.

Shirley and John worked for weeks on the endless red tape that would give them legal custody of Sandy. They talked to various authorities, made many phone calls, and wrote at least a dozen official letters.

Then one day a police officer came to check into the matter. His job was to see that Sandy was not a mere runaway who should be returned home. But Sandy didn't understand. "Policeman" meant only one thing to him: loss of freedom. And Sandy had to be free.

His old fears came rushing back. In those few moments, Sandy's new dreams were replaced by the old torments, distrust, and uncertainties. He did what seemed to be the story of his life—he ran away.

Shirley cried for days; John grieved as well.

Days passed with no word from Sandy. By faith, Shirley and John continued the adoption process. In the meantime, the Teen Challenge Girls Home in Los Angeles was suffering financially and was forced to close. The workers stood by helplessly, their hearts still burdened for the many unfortunate girls. Now they were not able to minister to any of them, and Sandy would have no place to run to in California.

Three months passed by. Then Sandy sent three postcards postmarked "Delano." One was addressed to Shirley and John, one to Mom Hall, and one to Marion. The cards were hopeless jumbles of words. Sandy had printed his message in capital letters in all directions, like a puzzle. Sentences crisscrossed each other. One deciphered card read:

> Sandy clean [free from drugs], Free [not in jail], Sandy loves you forever. Sandy eats three days [eats regularly], Sandy prays. Sandy misses you.

Another three months passed. Sandy was still "on the road." He went back to the Braddocks' home, but found no one there. John was holding services in California. When he and Shirley returned home, they found a paper bag inside the screen door. It contained food, money, and several paintings, at which Sandy had become quite proficient during his days at the girls' home. Some of the paintings depicted them; one was of Andraé and the choir. Sandy had scribbled several messages on the pictures, asking Shirley not to cry, letting them know he was still free from drugs, that he was OK, and that he loved and missed them very much.

More weeks went by. Then months. Sandy had no idea of how much time was passing. By Christmas, though, he was back on drugs and booze and worse off than ever. When he wasn't high, his mind was constantly on Shirley and John and on the Teen Challenge workers and Andraé Crouch. He managed to stay drunk or high almost twenty-four hours a day.

On the streets, Sandy still seemed more animal than human. His clothing smelled. His skin and tangled hair were filthy. He ate on his haunches and snarled like a wolf. His deafness brought out violent bitterness. Outwardly he seemed to fit the social worker's description—"human garbage."

Trapped inside that unapproachable exterior, however, was a very intelligent human being. Before, Sandy had been proud of himself for merely surviving. Now he knew that there was more to life than mere survival. Sandy knew he was not just alone—he was lonely.

Sandy was driven to futile attempts at forming new friendships. Once, in the San Francisco Bay area, Sandy wandered onto the grounds of a school for deaf children. He was so pleased to find boys and girls who were obviously like him—they talked with their hands! He hung around the grounds for days and eventually wandered into one of the classrooms.

The children were terrified of Sandy. However, an amazingly dedicated teacher, Mrs. Connie Forsgren, allowed Sandy to choose a desk and stay.

Sandy visited Mrs. Forsgren's class several times before the teacher was able to convince Sandy to come home with her. A divorcée, she lived with her teenaged son and daughter in Santa Clara. Sandy spent the night with the Forsgrens. It was only the first of many visits.

Mrs. Forsgren tried to trace Sandy's background but had little success. She recognized that she would have to have legal custody of Sandy in order to get "her" the medical help which Sandy desperately needed. Besides all of the drug-related problems, Sandy was now prone to epileptic seizures. The Forsgrens were good people who wanted to help, but Sandy knew that if he stayed long, a policeman would show up, just like the one who had come to the Braddocks. Sandy was convinced that he would be sent back to the mental hospital.

One day his phobia about the mental hospital and his desire for drugs overcame him. He searched the Forsgren house for money and jewelry and then left.

Afterwards, Sandy's conscience troubled him. Until then he'd never been plagued with a conscience. *What will Shirley and Marion say if they know what I've done? And Connie's been so good to me.* He wondered what Andraé would say.

Sandy was mad at himself. Now, on top of being lonely, he felt ashamed. But what could he do—he'd never be able to change. His despair was summed up in a letter he dictated via sign language and grunts to an old bum in San Francisco and sent to Shirley and the Teen Challenge workers. The writing style was determined primarily by the man who penned Sandy's communication:

It don't be easy how I have to live. I am all screwed up inside of me. It is too late for me, cause I have went too far in the way I am. It is right that you are here. You have did a lots of good. You all have given me what I not forget. It don't be easy to go in the streets. If I don't get the hell beat out of me, I maybe see you all someday. If it don't be that way, I want you guys to know I have something that

55

I did never have before. I may be split up
when you read this. It don't be easy to go and
say good-bye. I can't read it or write it. So
that is why I don't be able to write to none of
you. I don't forget it, your pretty house and
your pretty music. I have to split now.

                                Bye,
                                Sandy

P.S. There is so much food there and tasted
real good and you all the best cooks that have
ever been.

Sandy's letter reflected the loneliness and
despair of his life on the run. What it didn't
reveal was the extent of his physical and psycho-
logical deterioration. His sporadic visits to those
who had befriended him—Marion, Shirley and
John Braddock, Andraé Crouch, and Connie
Forsgren—were always met with joy and relief.
However, it was plain to them that Sandy was
becoming more alien and animallike than ever.

CHAPTER SIX

Sandy awoke with a startled jerk. Alone in the park on the outskirts of Oakland, he'd curled up against some shrubbery to sleep. But now, just on the other side of the bushes and only fifty feet away were more than a dozen members of a motorcycle gang.

The young teenager slid further into the greenery and then lay without moving a muscle. The men in black leather jackets had pulled in on the biggest bikes Sandy had ever seen. Sandy's deafness had made it impossible for him to hear them, although the throbbing motors had made the earth quake, jolting Sandy into consciousness.

Nothing brought more fear to his heart than bikers. In the late sixties and early seventies, Oakland had become headquarters for not only the Hell's Angels, but also for many other equally violent gangs. Sandy knew a person could get himself knifed just for looking at a gang member wrong. The only smart thing to do around "dudes" like that was to stay hidden.

Sandy hadn't meant to be spying on their activities, but his hiding place was so close to the clearing where they stood that he saw every detail. The insignias on the backs of their leather jackets were not familiar ones. He read each of the bearded faces clearly—cruel, scarred faces with reefers hanging from sneering lips.

The men were much older than Sandy, in their late twenties or early thirties. Their massive, muscle-bound arms could turn even a stick of wood into a lethal weapon. Several of the men were brandishing clubs. Some held knives and brass knuckles. One waved a jagged, broken beer bottle. They were grouped around a young, clean-cut man whom they had pulled off one of the motorcycles and thrown to the ground.

Suddenly the gang began beating the man. Whether the bikers had a reason to be angry with him or had picked him at random as a target for their drunken tempers, Sandy didn't know. His damaged ears heard none of their vile language. Whatever the motive, their torture of the young man continued for a long time. A very long time.

Sandy watched it all. He was street toughened: it never occurred to him to look away or to cover his eyes. Yet in all of his seven years on the streets, Sandy had never witnessed such demonic cruelty. The bikers maimed their victim and broke his bones. Blood was everywhere.

Just when Sandy thought they were finished

and would leave so that he could go for help, the men began to dig a shallow grave. They threw the tortured man in and then buried him alive. Sandy knew he was still alive when they buried him because Sandy caught a glimpse of the man's tear-drenched, terror-stricken eyes.

Then, before Sandy knew what was happening, rough hands grabbed his ankles and dragged him out from underneath the hedge. While his eyes had been glued to the tragedy before him, one of the bikers had been scouting the area for intruders and spied Sandy's scrawny legs sticking out of the bushes.

The furious biker pushed a struggling Sandy to the center of the mob. Everything else was forgotten as every eye was suddenly fixed on the cringing spy. A gang member raised a knife. Sandy realized that there could soon be two shallow graves in the clearing.

The leader of the group grabbed the arm of the man who held the knife. "Hold on, Nick!" he ordered. "I've seen this little Injun before. Sleeps in this park. She's crazy—pure loco— can't even talk good enough to squeal about what she's seen. No need to even finish off this piece of trash." The man with the knife angrily disagreed, but he obeyed his leader.

Instead of killing Sandy, they forced him onto one of the Harleys and drove him through Oakland before they dumped him on a secluded side street. Sandy sat rigidly in the gutter, still not knowing what they planned to do to him.

"Listen to me, Injun," the head man growled. "I know you can't say much. But if you ever speak even a word about what you've seen today, no matter where you go, I'll find you and cut your heart out."

Then he spat on Sandy and waved a gloved fist at the gang. They sped away in a cloud of fumes.

For days the memory of the murder was so vivid that Sandy could hardly sleep. Booze and dope only accentuated the event in his mind. Hallucinations haunted him. The visions always ended with the bikers cutting his heart out and throwing him into the grave beside their first victim.

"Don't speak a word of this," the monstrous figure in his memory warned him. *Don't speak a word of this,* he thought a hundred times each day.

What if I blab something out loud when I'm drunk or stoned? Sandy worried. He believed that any word spoken in the streets would somehow get back to the bikers. In his mind they were almost omnipresent. They would find him for sure.

Somehow the torment brought Sandy to a decision that even psychologists can't explain, a decision that went beyond Sandy's consciousness, penetrating his subconscious mind. The strength of the boy's will had always been uncanny, almost superhuman. Now Sandy called upon all the force of that will and decided, *I will not talk again.*

Sandy had always had trouble with his voice. (Years later, a doctor would discover that the scars on Sandy's neck were probably ice-pick wounds which had damaged the vocal cords when the boy was too young to even remember the incident.) Still, he could make sounds. But when Sandy decided, *I will not talk again,* he literally became mute. Psychosomatic effects took over. He no longer had to think, *I will not talk.* He actually couldn't talk. That was in September 1972.

Sandy would be virtually silent for almost eight years. Even then, he would utter only a single sentence.

NOVEMBER 1972

The damp coastal fog of the San Francisco Bay area pushed Sandy southward toward places he knew would keep him warm throughout the winter. For a few days, he stopped in the vicinity of a drug rehabilitation center in Santa Cruz. There Sandy had an encounter which would soften his heart, one that seemed hard as stone. He met Naomi Tanner, the founder of the Harvester Foundation Rehabilitation Center in Hidden Bay, Oregon. In her early thirties, the "preacher lady" was tall and vibrant. Her square face was well tanned and accented by a strong jawline that spoke strength of character. The power of her attractive face was softened by her wideset eyes—brown, flecked with gold.

Sandy conveyed in sign language this account of their meeting:

The woman called Naomi and I first met in Santa Cruz. I was out running close to the ocean like many times before. I was up to nothing, out drinking

*alone, walking around, looking for things to get
into. Jesus people came up to me and talked about
having many surprises to eat. They were telling
everybody to come on for a big-time meal [Thanks-
giving] over at the Center. I thought about eating.
It sounded OK.*

*We got into a van and drove to a big center, and I
walked in trying to pull myself together a little bit. By
this place on the beach, they were having music. I
saw a woman singing and playing a guitar and
talking.*

*After some time she looked down at me and gave
me a big Jesus smile. I looked back at her with a look
that said, "I don't believe you." I gave her one of
my many hard looks saying, "Back off, I don't want
to hear no preaching."*

*She kept singing, and in time I walked up to the
tall speakers so I could hear the music a little bit. I
didn't like preaching but I thought singing was OK.
I leaned on the speakers and thought,* This is not bad
for a preacher momma.

*Many street people came together at the meeting to
sing and eat. I got a plate, but it was hard walking
up to smiling people and having them put food on
it. The preacher momma finished singing. She saw me
and so I gave her one more big, dirty look. But
she walked over to me. She told me, "Would you like
to eat? Come on!" I followed her to those big tables
of food.*

*She made a big, big plate full of food—everything
that was there—and handed it to me. I thought
again,* Not too bad for a preacher momma, *but I
ate good!*

Many people in one place made me shy so I walked

as to leave when the lady asked if I had somewhere to sleep. I nodded yes and split.

I thought, Now I am one full, happy boy. So I went back down the beach to see what was up. The ocean was rolling. Sometimes there would be many surfers out and I would watch them ride high waves. I saw some drinking and they gave me beer. Beer and my full stomach did not go good, and in time I got real sick. But never did this make me think to stop drinking.

At about 11:00 P.M. it was time to go somewhere or the police would get me. I walked back to the Center and thought, I will sleep somewhere in that building. People walked out and told me free coffee was inside, so inside I went. I was feeling high and I always like coffee. But inside a big headache [seizure] came, and I remember nothing after that.

I didn't know then, but in time they told me someone went to the preacher momma and told her about me passing out and asked what to do. The momma said, "Bring her to my car and I will take her with me and see if we can help."

I don't remember, but she told me I woke up a minute and said, "I don't need help." Smashed out of my head but I thought I needed no help from a preacher lady. I don't know how she talked me into going to a motel with her and her children. I understand now that I gave her one hard time all that night. I have never felt good about sleeping in beds. They said I kept falling out all that night.

The momma thought I was just a young girl so she put her arms around me to keep me from throwing myself out of bed onto the floor. I remember waking up and thinking, Who's that? Many times before, I sleep by hippy friends after taking much "happy pop" [drugs], but I think, Who is this? I never seen this hair before.

The next day we were back at the Center for more singing and food. In two days time I remember the preacher momma telling me that the next day she was going up to her home faraway. I told myself, This is nothing to me, but I was crazy I was so sad about this lady going faraway. How friendly she was to me! She made me feel like I was not too bad a guy.

One thing I have thought about over and over was that in those three days she never told me I have to stop how I'm living like so many people had said to me before. Many had told me, "Stop this and this and this." She did not say those things. She treated me good like she treated anyone else. This strong feeling she gave me and I will never forget it.

In a little time it was time to say good-bye, so I walked over to her van. I tried to make like I didn't really care about preacher momma going bye-bye.

Then she gave me a smiling picture of her and showed me her name and address on the back. She told me she had many children like me at her big home and that I would be wanted there if I would come someday. Before I knew what I did, I took out my old harmonica that I had for so long and I gave it to her to remember me by. She got in the van and I waved like to say, "See you around."

Then, I did not know why I did this, but I made hand motions which said to her, "My eyes will see you again."

CHAPTER SEVEN

Naomi and Sandy would not meet again face to face for two years. From November 1972 to March 1974, their lives would be parallel in several ways. The stone child and the woman of steel would know loneliness, disappointment, and fear on one hand and friendship, hope, and joy on the other. And both would actually sustain severe physical pain incurred by ill health and violence at the hands of cruel people.

During that two-year interval, Sandy would return to some of the people who had shown him love and concern in previous months and years. He would think often of Marion Sweitzer, Faith, Andraé Crouch, Connie Forsgren, and the others who had already genuinely tried to help him.

Sandy's hearing also continued to worsen, making him more jittery when crossing streets and walking or hitchhiking along highways. Various additional brushes with oncoming traffic showed him how nearly total his deafness had become.

Sandy's seizures and spasms were growing increasingly frequent. He now had headaches that almost paralyzed him. Scars covered his entire body. And there was, in his mind, a gnawing fear that vengeful bikers would spot him wherever he was.

By the end of March 1974, Sandy felt that everyone had given up on him. He knew that they had a right to. Finally, he gave up on himself as the following account he signed graphically suggests:

For about two more Christmases after meeting Naomi, I was out running around, giving the police hell. Trying to fill up my days like I could still have a good time. Two families wanted to take me in [Braddocks and Mrs. Forsgren], but I had no papers and if they ever found any papers on me, they would have to give me back to the crazy place because Sandy had done many bad things. For this reason I would split and come together, split and come together with all the friends I had ever come to know.

I faced a very low, black-like-night time for me. I never knew a reason, but the headaches came worse and worse. When I had headaches, the police could catch me easy.

One night I was beat up in Santa Cruz and the police caught me. I didn't know why, but a good cop said, "We'll give you one more chance before we lock you up and throw away the key." They took me over to the Center. There was a man there who came up to me and said, "Are you the one they call Sandy?"

*When I told him yes, he said, "Do you remember a
preacher called Naomi? I'm from Oregon, where she
lives. She told me, 'If you run into a kid called Sandy,
tell her she can still come up and try living with us.' "*

I thought, This is all I can do, or I will kill myself
so they cannot lock me up back at that crazy
farm.

*I remembered that I had told that woman, "My
eyes will see you again." But I had not really believed
even in a good dream that this would really happen!*

*So, off we went to I-know-not-where—called
Oregon. I was thinking,* I hope that the preacher
momma is tough enough to stand me for a while.

Sandy didn't have any hope that Naomi would
keep him for long. After all, weren't the people
right who had told him, "You're hard inside like
a rock—like a child made of stone"?

CHAPTER EIGHT

APRIL 1974

"Naomi, you won't believe this, but we've just run into that girl named Sandy! I went to the Drug Misuse Prevention Center here in Santa Cruz to see if they had any information on her. They hadn't seen her since the Thanksgiving Outreach." Tom Higgins, supervisor of the men's division at the Harvester Foundation Rehabilitation Center, had taken the Foundation's singing group, The Oregonians, to sing at a beach rally in Santa Cruz. The rally was similar to the one at which Naomi had first met Sandy two years before.

"How is she?" Naomi asked eagerly, her golden brown eyes widening at the news.

"She's doing better," Tom said slowly.

"What do you mean?" Naomi sensed trouble.

"Well, while we were at the rehab center here, someone dumped Sandy's body in front of the building! She'd been badly beaten and stayed unconscious for hours. Her face looked like she'd seen a ghost. I don't know what could've happened. Anyway, I showed her your picture. She remembers you all right. I asked her if she wants to come to Oregon and see the 'preacher lady,' and she jumped at the chance. I guess we'll be bringing this little animal of a person home with us tomorrow.''

When she hung up the receiver, Naomi lay back on her pillow and groaned. "Oh, God, of all the times to find Sandy! You *know* we want to help the poor thing, but why *now?* I don't think I'm up to it, Lord! I *know* I'm not up to it!''

Yet the invitation had already been given and accepted. Sandy's coming was a foregone conclusion. Naomi closed her eyes and thought, *If you want to help someone, then you have to help them when they really need it, not just when it's convenient to you.* With that thought, she determined to open her home to the wild child whom she thought was a girl.

Her mind raced back to the events which had brought her to this place in time. The most immediate was the accident which had left her in a body brace and had forced her to stay practically bed-ridden.

In early March, Naomi, Tom Higgins, and an assistant, Claudia Nowton, had gone to Mexico in the Harvester Foundation's Dodge Van which pulled a U-Haul trailer. In Mexicali, they'd crammed the rented trailer with pottery, paintings, and leather goods with which to stock the Harvester Thrift Shop—an outgrowth of the Foundation's attempt to give rehabilitated drug addicts a chance to find work and develop self-worth.

North of Los Angeles, the van had passed a Mexican woman hitchhiking with her three small children and her aging mother, who had a withered arm. Tom stopped to give them a ride. During the long night's drive with kindhearted *gringos,* or "foreigners," the young woman named Lillia began to relax.

She told them she had been supporting her children and mother by working as a prostitute in East Los Angeles. She was just eighteen and desired to escape that way of life, but in crowded East L.A. she could not find a decent job. Lillia was heading north, thinking that if she lived in an area with less population, there would surely be some sort of decent work for her.

"Are you willing to wash dishes and wait on tables?" Naomi asked her.

"Yes, of course," Lillia told them.

Tom invited Lillia to travel to Oregon with them and offered her a trial job at the Taco Fiesta Café, another outgrowth of the Foundation's ministry. Naomi offered one of the unfinished bedrooms as a temporary shelter for her and her family. Responding gratefully as if a golden mansion had been opened to her, the young Mexican gladly accepted their offer.

By 4:00 A.M. the van neared Willows, California. Tom was driving, and Claudia and Lillia were with him in the front seat. Naomi stretched out in back with the three children and their grandmother to sleep until dawn. They seemed to be the only ones on the road in those early morning hours.

Suddenly, as if from out of nowhere, a semi-truck roared down upon them at eighty miles an hour, crossed from the left lane, and struck them broadside. The force of the impact was so great that the van flew up in the air and landed on the nose of the semi. Tossed from the trailer like a toy, the Dodge rolled four times and landed upright along the shoulder of the freeway.

The tangle, terror, and confusion inside the vehicle were indescribable. Miraculously, the van had rolled so quickly that the roof did not cave in and crush the eight people inside. All of the wheels were demolished, every window shattered, and the roof dented in the middle. Where the top of the van had been inverted, a slab of metal had pressed down into the vehicle and crashed in on Naomi.

She never lost consciousness. When the van stopped rolling, she immediately began to check on the others. Her scalp had been cut open, her spine rammed and crushed, and she was in shock. She thought the blood covering the quilts was from one of the children.

"Let's get out. It may blow!" Tom yelled and picked up the little grandmother. Naomi scrambled out via the back doors, pulling the children with her.

Away from the vehicle and in the light of the moon, the group could see what a bloody mass Naomi was. Lillia screamed and Claudia dropped to her knees, groaning. All the adults prayed loudly and fervently. Naomi was covered with blood from head to foot; literal streams of scarlet ran from her feet onto the concrete.

A police car and an ambulance arrived in only minutes. Hours later when Naomi opened her eyes, she found herself in the intensive care unit of the Garden City General Hospital.

Doctors at the hospital knew that Naomi had lost so much blood so quickly that it wasn't humanly possible for her to have survived. "Her bloodstream surely was almost dry," an incredulous Dr. Whitney told Tom. As transfusion after transfusion was given, the deep slash on her skull was sewn tight.

After her stay in the hospital, Naomi was taken home to Harbour County Hospital where she remained for three more weeks. She began to heal internally. Dozens of X-rays prompted the doctors to forego back surgery, at least for the time being. But she would need to wear a brace, day and night.

The brace was a total body-support system. It fit from the tip of her spine to up around her shoulders and neck; there was a chin support for the weight of her head. The straps prevented Naomi from turning her neck to either the right or the left. Even a very slight movement would bring on severe nausea and vomiting. Only Tom and Claudia knew that the brace might be needed for years.

Three weeks before Easter, Naomi was allowed to go home. Naomi, her children, her church, and the Center workers were ecstatic. On her homecoming day, Naomi's faith soared. The mighty God who had preserved her life could easily take care of the head wound and the twisted spine.

Meanwhile, the others involved in the terrifying collision were back to work at the Harvester Foundation, although it was a long time before all of the bandages and bruises were gone. Lillia was working hard as a waitress, and she, her babies, and her mother were living in Naomi's home.

Naomi began to trust God for a complete healing, especially since she had already seen the Lord heal drug addicts and twisted minds. Because she lived with pain, she learned to ask for faith to endure moment by moment. On Easter Sunday, in an act of total trust, she left her room to preach the Easter sermon at her church, Faith Tabernacle.

As she stood in the pulpit, she silently prayed for strength. She talked without notes and had to rely on her memory of the Scriptures because it was impossible for her to look down to read. The sanctuary was jammed. The congregation agreed it was the most powerful message they had ever heard.

"Sometimes it seems we must watch the death of our dearest dreams and ambitions," she told them. "But often it is only through crushing and death that there can be a resurrection! Through times which seem like 'death,' we find a doorway to resurrection power. We move from natural living to the supernatural!"

Though she was growing better, the brace still kept Naomi immobile. Most of her time was spent in her room.

Naomi had, nevertheless, been exerting her leadership in the drug rehabilitation program. That included keeping track of the Taco Fiesta Café and the thrift shop operated by the young people the Foundation was helping. Much of her time was also spent enjoying visits from the "Walton-itros," her growing family of adopted children—Billy, Robert, David, Manuel, Victor, Rosa, and Miguel—and from her co-workers and the teenagers living on the Foundation grounds.

The "Walton-itros" cared for "Momma" in ways that were often hilarious. As she rested or sat stiffly in bed, they brought her dozens of gifts. Billy somehow felt that frogs in the room would speed her recovery, and loving little Robert brought in bouquet after bouquet of weeds.

Throughout each day, first one young head and then another would quietly peek into the bedroom. No child was ever told to go away, no matter how severely in pain Naomi was at the moment. In a few weeks those visits between Naomi and her adopted children built bridges of understanding that years of a normal relationship might never have accomplished. Naomi gratefully acknowledged God's hand in this, the most important area of her life.

Even Claudia, concerned over the "pestering," had to admit that the hilarious efforts of the youngsters were speeding Naomi's recovery.

Being almost flat on her back also gave Naomi time to reminisce and reflect on her life and ministry. Thirty-five years old and unmarried, she'd already experienced life intensely. "To think I once thought to myself, *I'll have a normal lifestyle!*" Naomi mused out loud. Looking back, she realized that she had *never* had a normal lifestyle.

PART TWO

NAOMI
Woman
of Steel

TOP: The Tanner family in 1946: (seated) Mel;
Lorene Tanner; her husband, Eli; Naomi;
(standing) Melba and Nina
BOTTOM: Naomi at age fourteen—hardened by
her brother Mel's death and headed for trouble

CHAPTER ONE

EARLY BACKGROUND: 1939–1963

Naomi's lifestyle had never been what most people consider "normal." Her father, Eli, had been an expert lumberjack, lugging his family from mill camp to mill camp. Naomi's mother, Lorene, always made a home for her husband and their five children in the small cabins which usually lacked running water and electricity.

Eli and Lorene had met and gotten married in Iowa but moved to the mountains of Oregon in the thirties so that Eli could become a lumberjack. Early in their marriage they'd discovered the faith that set them apart from the majority of the people who worked among the tall timber. The two were loved, respected, and approached for their advice.

When Naomi was born—in November 1939—there were already four other children: Melba, aged ten; Melvin, aged seven; Nina, aged five;

and baby Avery, who later died of pneumonia at two-and-a-half. Even as an infant, Naomi was exceptionally bright and inquisitive. She also had a strong will.

"Strength of character is a good thing in a child," Eli would tell Lorene. "Those are the ones who can get in big trouble, but they are also the ones who can bring the world the biggest blessings."

Young Naomi never doubted the reality of the Christian faith—the one she had heard proclaimed in the styles of a dozen denominations outside the mill camps. And there was just too much evidence of it in her home. "I don't have religion. I have Jesus," her father, Eli, had said.

Despite little formal schooling, Eli would read the Bible out loud every night, slowly sounding out the words and following each line with his massive, calloused fingers. Lorene was able to memorize Scripture easily, often learning entire chapters as she went about her chores. She'd repeat them to Eli and the children at night.

In 1949 when Naomi was ten, her family settled in the small coastal town of Hidden Bay, Oregon. They made a permanent home in a large, two-story frame house at the edge of the pine-scented forest. Eli established a business of his own as a mechanic.

That was the happiest year Naomi had ever known because her older brother, Mel, became her best friend. Mel was very adept at boxing and began to teach Naomi the basics of sparring. Her parents saw nothing wrong with it since Naomi was already quite feminine.

After a while, Naomi began to get in a few good punches. Sometimes she'd take a tumble from a particularly strong, but playful, jab from Mel and would cry. "Don't whimper, Naomi, or I'll stop teaching you. A person has to learn to get up when they're knocked down instead of having a self-pity party," Mel would always say. Naomi must have heard that a hundred times. His advice would come in handy later on in her life. Only hindsight would prove those words prophetic.

In 1951, the family was struck by the sudden, tragic death of Mel. At twenty he had recently married his high school sweetheart and had won the amateur lightweight-boxing championship for Oregon. Then someone challenged him to a fight when he and a few buddies were out on the town. Mel didn't want to fight, but the drunken insults became more and more vile. When Mel started toward one of the men, the man pulled out a gun and shot Mel at point-blank range. Mel died instantly.

His death plunged the entire family into despair. Lorene and Eli no longer acted like normal, let alone strong, people. At Christmas, Lorene allowed no tree in the home, no presents, or any form of celebration. She'd lost her first son in infancy and now her other son in the prime of his life. Her nerves were frayed, and her three daughters found it impossible to be around her. Eli became a workaholic. At home, he was quiet and withdrawn, and stared into space for hours. They still had faith, but their hearts were scarred.

The oldest daughter, Melba, got married, leaving Naomi and Nina alone to cope with their own grief, as well as that of their parents. The strain was too much for them. The girls reacted by avoiding home altogether and began to run the streets.

Naomi, especially, seemed bound for trouble. After all, Mel had taught her how to box. Growing strong and healthy and as tall as her father, she began to use that skill.

Subconsciously she felt that boxing was an inheritance from Mel, a way to remember him. Both Naomi and Nina began drinking and running with older crowds. Reports began to get back to Eli and Lorene from the high school that Naomi was actually *fighting*. At the slightest provocation, Naomi punched out not only girls, but also boys her own age.

It was more than simply a matter of skill. For Naomi, it was her steel will that her parents always spoke of—this time, reinforced by a terrible bitterness.

Eli and Lorene slowly realized what some people never do: if they continued to grieve over their loss, they would lose what they had left. Thus, they sought God's help for the heaviness that still permeated their household after three years and had driven the girls to the streets.

"Many mothers have lost sons," Lorene said. "Mine were lost to me temporarily, but I've begun to see them as eternal beings, safe with Jesus, whom I will see again. And under my roof are two daughters who are also eternal creatures.

I have to begin to take care of the inner souls of my girls.''

Bridges to children aren't rebuilt quickly, but the Tanners began to try. The walls and barriers, especially with Naomi, seemed insurmountable; they had to be knocked down.

Eli began to spend all the time with her that he could. He even took her to his shop and showed her the basics of auto mechanics. He tried to interest her in using her natural athletic coordination in a sport which could become a career: women's basketball or track. Naomi would have none of it.

At fifteen, Naomi was jailed for stealing a car. In desperation, the Tanners let Naomi and Nina live with a young friend from their church, Carol Harrison. They felt the girls had to see faith working in someone other than their parents.

Carol became a trusted friend to whom Naomi could pour her heart out. She learned from Carol that probably the greatest gift one can give a hurting, young heart is time. Naomi began to confide the secrets of her heart, even sharing with Carol the constant suicidal thoughts which plagued her.

Living in Carol's home made little difference to Naomi who continued to drink and to run the streets. Strong cords of love were pulling her to a better way of life, but she felt sure she could withstand them. As long as she and Nina had each other, she thought, they could resist any persuasive arguments.

One night Carol and the Tanners drove Nina

and Naomi to a church service. Sullen and angry, the girls listened as the pastor spoke about people who deliberately harden their hearts to the love of God.

That night as she lay on her bed at Carol's, it was all Naomi could do to keep from telling Nina that she was tired of hardening her heart. She felt as if an invisible net were wrapping itself around her, pulling her away from the crowd she had been running with. But how could she tell Nina? Her sister would only laugh sarcastically.

Suddenly Nina spoke through the darkness. "Naomi, I've had it. I don't want to let you down, but I'm going to have to give my heart to the Lord. I'm tired of rebelling against his ways. That's why there is so much trouble in this world. People rebel and they get mean and then they hurt people like that man hurt our Mel. I don't want to turn into someone like that—a destroyer."

Naomi heard a soft thud as Nina slid out of bed and knelt in the stillness of the summer night. With a sob, Naomi got to her knees beside her sister, and both girls began to pray.

For the next few days, Naomi devoured the Bible with the same hunger that she had seen in her parents. *How can they be so thirsty for the Word of God?* she used to wonder. Now she knew. As she read, tears began to flow, tears that she had stifled for three years ever since Mel had been killed. And with the tears came healing. In her reading, Naomi found a verse that boggled her mind:

> *Seeing then that we have a high priest, . . . Jesus the Son of God, . . . not a high priest which cannot be touched with the feeling of our infirmities; but was in all points tempted like as we are, yet without sin.*
>
> (Hebrews 4:14, 15)

As she wept, Naomi felt that Jesus was weeping with her. Contrary to the distant, vindictive God she had imagined, she discovered the High Priest who can "be touched," who was approachable and understanding.

Naomi's conversion at age sixteen had been genuine, a total turning of her will toward God. She had grown spiritually very quickly, and intended to go to seminary or Bible college.

Invitations to speak began pouring in, and she was eager to share her testimony. A witty, dynamic speaker, Naomi also sang and played the guitar. Because of her solid home training, she had a firmer grasp of Scripture than did some people many years her senior. Naomi quickly became a favorite speaker for youth groups all over the country.

In 1956 Naomi met Evelyn King, another young believer who sang beautifully and played the guitar. Evelyn had had a horrible childhood, been married at fifteen, and had two babies. Then her husband was imprisoned for armed robbery and promptly decided to forget her and the children.

To look at Evelyn, one would never have imagined her past. The gospel had transformed her completely. She was fresh and radiant, a living example that *if any man be found in Christ, he is a new creature: old things pass away; behold, all things become new.*

(2 Corinthians 5:17)

Naomi and Evelyn became fast friends and decided to travel together for a "short time." Along with them went Evelyn's children, little Ricky and Darlene. Naomi became their "Aunt Naomi."

Both Naomi and Evelyn took Bible correspondence courses from Springs of Living Water. In 1958, because of their fine ministry and obvious calling, they were ordained.

For a while after their ordination, they team-pastored an Indian mission church in "the back side of the desert" in Trinidad, California. They accepted the position because the ministry to thirty adults and many children had had no teacher for years. The experiences Naomi and Evelyn had matured them.

The "short time" stretched into ten years. The women sang together so well that they were in constant demand, especially for summer youth camps and the big Youth for Christ rallies prominent in the fifties and early sixties. As Darlene and Ricky grew, they showed tremendous musical talent and often took part in special numbers.

The most difficult times, the times that built spiritual muscle, were the years on the road. Crisscrossing America many times in their camper-van, the young evangelists learned the reality of "walking by faith."

"It does *not* mean mooching off of people," they decided early in their partnership. For the first few years, they would hardly accept an offering. When ministering in an area, they earned money by doing odd jobs such as picking fruit in the fields. "After all, the Apostle Paul sometimes earned money by mending tents!" Naomi would grin. They took Ecclesiastes 9:10 as their guide:

Whatsoever thy hand findeth to do, do it with thy might.

They also knew that one of the Old Testament Hebrew names for God was *Jehovah-Jireh*, which translated means "God will provide."

In 1962, the team went home to Oregon. After just a few weeks, so many adults in Naomi's hometown of Hidden Bay were converted that a church was born. Naomi and Evelyn couldn't leave the new believers and no pastors were available. So in 1963, "Faith Tabernacle" was incorporated and the women began their second pastorate. Thanks to the building experts in the fellowship, they were able to move into a pleasant sanctuary.

After many years on the road, they made Hidden Bay their permanent home. Eli and Lorene welcomed the women into their large frame home. Naomi carried most of the preaching load for the growing church; Evelyn, the office work and Christian education.

CHAPTER TWO

1963–1967

"I should have never taken as my motto the verse that says: *Whatsoever thy hand findeth to do, do it with thy might,*" Naomi said laughingly. "I just had no idea how much my hands would find to do!"

Besides pastoring a church, she had the adjustment required of a woman as pastor. While she loved drawing from the truths of the Word and applying them to daily life, she found the challenge of the ministry often emotionally overwhelming.

When making hospital calls, she'd experience physical pain as part of the empathy she felt with the patients she visited. Funerals were equally difficult for her. Handling situations involving child abuse or incest shook her to the core.

"The congregation will have to find another

pastor," she decided. The church, however, wanted Naomi, not a new pastor. And Naomi knew that she was following God's will for her life.

Gradually, she adjusted to the weight of pastoral responsibility. As she came to rely on the resources of God, she discovered that his wisdom and love never ran out. She also began to realize one of the purposes for which the Holy Spirit had been given: to give spiritual power.

In 1965, Naomi's household began to fill up with children. In addition to Evelyn's growing children, Evelyn's brothers, Mike and Danny, were placed in the custody of Naomi and Evelyn. (Their parents were alcoholics.) The children remained with the two women for several years.

As Naomi's reputation as a "miracle worker" with troubled teens grew, a social worker approached her about being a foster parent for the Becker children—Wanda, sixteen; David, fifteen; and Sharon, thirteen. The siblings remained in her care until they graduated from high school. Another foster daughter, beautiful, orphaned Marlis McClure, joined them.

In view of their growing "clan," Eli, Lorene, Evelyn, Naomi, and the eight teenagers moved into a massive eight-bedroom turn-of-the-century "mansion," complete with a well-worn winding staircase and a round bedroom. In the old home of a nineteenth-century ship captain, the group felt like a "ragtag Waltons' TV show."

At bedtime, the household laughingly imitated that TV family's nightly routine:

"Goodnight, Mike-Boy!"

"Goodnight, David-Bob!"

"Goodnight, Wanda-Ellen!"

"Goodnight, everyone!" Naomi would finally yell.

"This situation is *different,"* Evelyn reminded Naomi. "Our teens have had terrible problems, but at least we can *talk* to them. This is a *baby.* Helping her will take *hours....*" Evelyn stopped mid-sentence as Naomi unwrapped the tiny girl she had brought home from the Department of Social Services. Five-month-old Shirley was a beautiful child with dark, curly hair, and saucer-like blue eyes. But the eyes were unresponsive, glass marbles which stared into space. The baby was limp on Naomi's lap.

"She isn't retarded," Ann McKenzie had told them. "The doctors say this infant's been so emotionally abused that she's in a state of shock. She may never develop normally. She *certainly* has no hope of coming out of it unless she receives special love and care. In this state, no family can be expected to adopt her. Naomi, your home is her only hope.... We can't just let her lie in a hospital bed."

"I'll try it for a few days," Naomi had conceded. "That's all we can promise."

The first time Naomi changed her diaper, she held the tiny feet in the air to powder Shirley and then reached for a pin. When she turned back to Shirley, the little legs were still suspended in the air. The motionless trance continued until Naomi pressed the little legs down onto the changing table. That pattern continued each time Shirley was changed.

When she was laid down to sleep, Shirley would remain in one position until someone turned her. She would eat, but she chewed and swallowed mechanically like a mindless, little robot or windup toy.

Pediatricians told Naomi that perhaps the infant had been beaten into total passivity and obedience. She had apparently been clothed, fed, and placed in the crib but had received no cuddling or affection.

The "few days" to which Evelyn and Naomi had committed themselves stretched into weeks and months. After a "Walton-style conference" the household hit upon a simple treatment plan: taking turns at cuddling and holding Shirley. Naomi told the teenagers, "We'll rock her, sing to her, and dangle toys in front of her. Whenever you get home from school, go right to the baby and greet her. We'll keep it up even if we don't see a response."

It took six months before Shirley's eyes began to follow the members of the family as they walked across the room. Then her eyes began responding to a toy. Gradually, her arms and legs began to stretch and wiggle. She learned to raise her head.

By Christmas, the tree lights elicited sounds of pleasure from her. Ann McKenzie periodically checked on Shirley's progress. Shirley was obviously growing normally.

That experience taught Naomi an amazing lesson: troubled teens need to help those more troubled than themselves. Never had the household run more smoothly than during this time. Naomi discovered that those who are down-and-out need to reach out. That principle became the foundation for the rest of Naomi's approach to ministry.

CHAPTER THREE

JANUARY 1968–OCTOBER 1970

Up to this point, Naomi had been a *foster* mother.
She'd loved and helped several children, only to
see them leave her home and be adopted by
someone else. The separations were becoming
harder to cope with.

"Ann, I want to *adopt* this one," Naomi told
Ann McKenzie, the social worker at the Department of Social Services. "I believe that it's God's
will that I adopt Ricky. And I have several other
good reasons too!"

Ann tried to be sympathetic to Naomi's
request, making it clear how unlikely the
adoption would be since she would be applying
as a single parent.

At the court hearing the judge found Naomi
"extremely competent" to adopt a child. Ricky's
father was ready to sign the release, but his
natural mother had a sudden change of heart.

She'd moved to Washington and had filed to regain custody of the child. "It's out of our jurisdiction," the judge told Naomi. "In Washington, natural parents have even more rights than here."

The judge closed the file and adjourned the hearing. Ricky was gone.

All Naomi could do was pray and grieve—not simply out of personal loss, but for the beautiful toddler who would be returning to a home which had already abused him terribly. When his natural parents had dumped him off at Naomi's house, Ricky was bruised from head to toe. The few times they'd merely approached him there, he had screamed until he hyperventilated.

Naomi felt spiritually and physically ill for several weeks. Then on top of the severe disappointment of losing Ricky, she became the victim of malicious gossip. Someone in her hometown of Hidden Bay had incorrectly deduced that since she hadn't been able to adopt Ricky, "the courts must have discovered she is a lesbian." The words hit her like a poisoned arrow.

She'd lived an exemplary life and had thought her reputation in the community a good one. Evelyn, her longtime co-worker, couldn't have been more of a sister to her than if she'd been a flesh-and-blood relation.

Then, although there was absolutely no basis for the rumor, several people from her congregation left "just to be cautious."

The question *why* raged in Naomi's mind. Why

would people who didn't even know her say such things? Why couldn't she get over the loss of Ricky? Why had the crazy lesbian rumor ever gotten started?

In the solitude of her own room, Naomi began getting some answers. Through Bible reading and prayer, she sensed the Holy Spirit telling her:

Ricky opened your heart to the possibility of adoption. You weren't willing to consider that ministry before. Wait and see what I do with that desire. And as to the rumors, they bother you so badly because for once in your life, you can't fight for yourself. You must begin to let me be your defender. This rumor is so hurtful because you can't "box" your way out of gossip and you know you're helpless.

The words from Hebrews—Jesus is the high priest that "can be touched"—also comforted her. "They hated me without a cause," Jesus had said in the Gospels. Despite slander and ridicule, Jesus had continued to walk the road of ministry.

If Naomi tried to accomplish anything with her life, if she dared to do anything even slightly unusual such as being a single parent, it would also entail some conflict, risk, maybe gossip, and probably some enemies.

Am I willing to take the risk? she asked herself. Taking a deep breath, she made her decision. Anything was better than a life of hiding, of wrapping hurt and resentment around herself like a blanket.

In 1970 Naomi made her first visit to an orphanage called "Los Niños" near Ensenada, Mexico. The Reverend and Mrs. Jess Brewer had founded it several years before and had often invited Naomi to visit. "We desperately need the prayer and financial support of congregations like yours. Won't you come and see firsthand what God is allowing us to do?" they had encouraged her.

When she arrived at the humble complex of clay buildings stretched out on the desert, she immediately felt at home. About thirty children from two to twelve years of age ran out to meet her. A few clung to her hands and skirt. "Looks like several have chosen you for their momma!" Jess Brewer teased. His words turned out to be prophetic.

Naomi stayed for two weeks. Her hands were full, working in the kitchen, teaching the children, and putting them to bed. She decided to ask her church board to give Los Niños monthly aid. She also measured the boys and girls for the Christmas clothes the housewives at her church would be happy to sew.

At the end of her stay, Naomi turned to Mrs. Conrique, the Mexican nurse who helped the Brewers. "Would you let me adopt one, maybe even two, of these children?" she asked.

That question opened the door to an extensive adoption ministry. Within a few weeks, Naomi would adopt nine-year-old Rosa; her eleven-year-old brother, Manuel; and a sad-eyed toddler named David Esperez. While Naomi's mind told her that adopting children was pure insanity, her heart told her that the decision was sensible and most of all, *right*.

Yes, she was in her thirties, single, and not well-to-do. Added to the challenge of adopting three children was the fact that they spoke no English and she spoke no Spanish. Still, she believed she was doing God's will for her life.

Back in Oregon, she met the director of the immigration office, Joseph Greene, a kind and gracious man. He was puzzled about how to handle the Mexican orphans. "I'll set up a special file for your children," he told Naomi, "until we know how to obtain permanent papers. Because of our problems with migrant workers and illegal aliens, the Mexican-American border situation is in a constant state of change."

The "settling in" process for the three children went surprisingly easy. The two older ones, Manuel and Rosa, picked up enough words from Naomi's foster children and Sunday school classmates to begin school in the fall. Little David quickly cast aside his few Spanish words and learned English without any trace of an accent.

Naomi and Evelyn with the first
three adopted children: Rosa, David,
and Manuel

CHAPTER FOUR

My hands are full, Naomi told herself. *All the foster children are grown now, but I have three of the most energetic children God ever created, plus the care of the church.*

She was happy and satisfied. Then in the winter of 1970, she felt she had to do something more.

The days of the radical hippy movement were drawing to a close, but the impact of the drug revolution on American young people was just beginning. Naomi read many articles about teenaged addicts. She saw documentaries on the drug problems in such cities as New York, Los Angeles, and San Francisco.

"But that can't be happening *here.* Not in such a small, conservative community as Hidden Bay, or can it?" she asked herself out loud.

At night, after housework and when Evelyn

and the children were asleep in bed, Naomi would get into her car and slowly drive through the streets of town. She began meeting a segment of her area's population that she hadn't even known existed.

Hidden Bay *did* have young drug users. There *were* teenaged alcoholics, and even teenaged prostitutes—pretty girls trapped in a web of drug habits too expensive to support any other way. Some were drifters "on the road." Most were local kids—nice kids.

Naomi was labeled a "square" by all of them. She was an "old lady" who never "turned on." But she didn't condemn. She wasn't aloof. She didn't "preach." Apparently she cared and wanted to be a friend.

Gradually, the subculture accepted her. Sometimes, after giving a teenager a ride or buying one a Coke at the only all-night hamburger hangout, she would be invited to a party.

The more she saw, the more troubled she became. How could she do anything about the situation? *These kids need love, understanding, and most of all, the power of the gospel to break them free from the drugs that bind them,* she thought. But she couldn't take them *all* into her home. God knew it was crowded enough now!

One day, someone gave her a flyer on "Teen Challenge," the drug rehabilitation center which David Wilkerson had founded in the slums of New York City. "Oh, no!" she whispered. "Why did I even *read* this thing?"

In November 1971, with the help of her congregation and the scorn of many community leaders, Naomi established the Harvester Foundation Rehabilitation Center. She leased an old grade school.

"We don't need this!" townspeople argued. Before the month was over, it became filled with twenty young, local addicts.

Naomi was not only a pastor and the mother of three growing children, but also now the director of an expanding nonprofit organization.

As the Foundation began to fill up with young exdrug addicts and alcoholics, Naomi clearly saw that the young men and women needed more than good food and a place to stay, more than wholesome recreation and even loving counsel. They needed a sense of responsibility; they needed to be needed. She remembered the surprising harmony that had come among her teenaged foster children when they had gladly accepted the responsibility of caring for Shirley and Ricky when they were toddlers.

To keep the Foundation from being solely dependent on donations, but *mainly* to give the teenagers self-worth, Naomi opened the Harvester Thrift Shop and the Taco Fiesta Café. Added to the weight of her other tasks, she was now the manager of a small store and often the head chef of a restaurant.

Both small enterprises thrived. The shop specialized in used furniture and clothing and also sold macrame objects, pottery, and other crafts the Harvester residents made. Because of her acquaintances in Mexico, Naomi was able to import Mexican crafts for the young people to sell. The restaurant served the only Spanish food around for miles. Because Naomi, Evelyn, and the several young people they trained were excellent cooks, the place was never empty.

Usually Naomi didn't get to bed until the early hours of the morning. Her arms and back always ached. Her head throbbed with a myriad of business details, but she believed she had tapped in on the same source of joy experienced by the famous Sister Theresa in India. Sister Theresa had written:

> People talk about my sacrifice. I have sacrificed nothing. I am the happiest person on earth. To give yourself to the needy, the poorest of the poor—this is the beginning of joy.

Without knowing it, without ever putting it into words, Naomi had followed another principle expressed by Sister Theresa:

> Why are people so afraid of one small child or of one broken person? We will never turn *anyone* away.

For Naomi, there was always room for one more—in the Center, in her home, and in her heart.

In April 1972, Naomi went to Mexico to purchase a truckload of Mexican crafts to be sold at the thrift shop. Since her permit required that she spend a night in Mexico, she decided to visit the orphanage to tell how beautifully Rosa, Manuel, and David were flourishing. While there, she felt drawn to adopt two more children, Billy and Victor, both around six years old. The paperwork for them took three weeks.

The following November, 1972, Naomi was asked to speak and sing at the Thanksgiving Beach Festival in Santa Cruz, California. It turned out to be the worst time for her to leave. Her household was crowded with her adopted children, including the new additions, Billy and Victor. She was also scheduled to meet with Joseph Greene, the sympathetic immigration official.

Owen Young, the organizer of the Festival, had been a member of Naomi's congregation, so Naomi felt a special obligation to accept the invitation. Owen's work in Santa Cruz had been impressive, and he had been named Man of the Year for the entire country in 1972. It would be hard to turn him down. Most of all, something in her heart compelled Naomi to go and she did.

While onstage before the masses of young people gathered on the Santa Cruz beach, Naomi noticed an Indian teenager. She couldn't tell whether he was actually male or female. What struck her besides the scrawny appearance was the fact that he stood with one ear pressed against the blaring loudspeakers while Naomi was playing the electric guitar. After the program, she tried to locate the Indian whom people said was a girl named Sandy.

When she finally located Sandy, Naomi looked into the face of what she considered the most miserable young person she had ever met. Her heart went out to Sandy, and she took special pains to see that he was given generous helpings of the sumptuous Thanksgiving dinner provided free for those attending the festival.

When it came time for Naomi to leave for her home in Oregon, she gave Sandy her name and address and encouraged him to come and visit her family. Sandy in turn gave her his treasured harmonica. Naomi was deeply touched. As they parted, Sandy signed to her the words, "My eyes will see you again."

Will I ever really see Sandy again? Naomi wondered as she left. *Is there any way someone can reach Sandy?*

CHAPTER FIVE

DECEMBER 1972–MARCH 1974

The timing of events in the mystery of God's will often leaves his children wondering *Why?* In the case of Sandy and Naomi, it is obvious that their first meeting on the beach at Santa Cruz had not been merely coincidental. Yet, why would they have to wait *two years* before meeting again?

Why would Sandy have to undergo even greater hardship and become more animallike than ever before? As Part One reveals, the period between November 1972 and March 1974 was a rollercoaster ride for Sandy, marked by heights of brief and poignant happiness and depths of progressively increasing pain and alienation.

Naomi, meanwhile, would adopt more children and see her Foundation ministry prosper, despite community disapproval and sinister threats. She, like Sandy, would experience dark nights of the soul.

Rejoice with them that do rejoice, Naomi read and winced, thinking how ironic that Bible passage seemed. The words of Romans 12:15 stung her to the core for one very good reason: it was Evelyn's wedding day.

"But God, how can I rejoice?" Naomi cried out loud. She knew she was complaining more than praying. *Evelyn and I've worked together for years. What will I do without her in the house to help with all these kids? I'll be terribly lonesome! I need an answer, God!*

Because you're jealous. The answer came quickly, but it was not one she was prepared to accept. Jealous? She started to protest, knowing it was useless. Yes, she was jealous, painfully jealous, but not over the man Evelyn was going to marry. Naomi was envious of a relationship of deep love.

Her own life had known accomplishment and a measure of fulfillment, but no abiding love between her and a man. She longed, at times desperately, for a strong husband who would be a good father to the children. There had been no real love in her life since Michael O'Leary when she was sixteen.

She'd often wondered what had become of the tall, husky man with dark, wavy hair and a crooked grin that reminded her of her dead brother Mel. She had been sixteen and he, twenty, when he'd given her an engagement ring.

Even though he was a Roman Catholic, he'd never insisted that she convert to his church.

"Don't worry about me, Hon," he had told her. "I believe in Jesus. It don't matter to me what church we go to. You go ahead and choose."

Maybe that's what's bothering me, she had thought after the engagement. Somehow, she hadn't felt the excited joy she thought she really should have as someone about to be married. *Is it his wishy-washy attitude about spiritual things that disturbs me?* But how could she hold that against him? She'd come to know the Lord only a few months earlier.

"Do you love him 100 percent, Naomi?" her wise father had asked her. No, not 100 percent. So, painful as it was, she had to break the engagement. It seemed the right thing for her and for Michael.

Eleven years later, Naomi heard that he had died in a racing car accident. There had been other men in her life. During the traveling years she had corresponded with many fine Christian men.

In 1965 she'd met Lonnie Reynolds, a service-man converted in one of the Faith Tabernacle services. She thought of Lonnie as a brother and was always careful about not seeing him outside a group. Nevertheless, Lonnie quickly grew serious and proposed. Once again, Naomi went through the turmoil and guilt of saying no to someone who loved her. The following year, he was transferred to a base in Europe.

That same year, Naomi's household had begun to fill up with children. *That really discouraged suitors!* Naomi thought, half laughing. The children had indeed consumed her time and energy so that she had had no extra time to think about romance.

Her thoughts returned to the reality of Evelyn's marriage scheduled to take place later in the day. "Oh, Father," she whispered, "Forgive me. Please *help* me!"

As she prayed, waves of peace began to wash over her soul, pushing her from the grip of jealousy.

With her own heart at peace, Naomi was free to think about Evelyn's first heartbreaking marriage to a violent man who had ended up in prison. She recalled Evelyn's years of faithful service to the Lord and her patience in raising Darlene and Ricky. Naomi would have to learn to adjust to the change of not having Evelyn around. But hadn't God already sent Naomi an answer ahead of time in the form of Claudia Nowton and Patsy? Their arrivals had not been chance events!

Claudia Nowton, a fine Christian woman, had arrived at the Foundation only the month before and had offered her services in whatever area she could be the most help. That area was with the children. Like Evelyn, Claudia was also an excellent cook and housekeeper. The "hodge-podge Waltons" adopted her into the family immediately.

Another young woman named Patsy had also joined the household ministry. She had been an amazing Christian as a teenager, a gifted soloist featured across the nation at the large Youth for

Christ rallies which were very effective in the early sixties. However, she had let her faith grow cold; her lifestyle, compromising. She'd withdrawn from Christian circles and in a few years became a slave to hard drugs.

Patsy ended up at the Harvester Foundation, where Naomi and the others were able to help restore her physically and spiritually. Now she'd become one of their most dynamic counselors.

Claudia and Patsy had already been such a help to the family and the Center. *The Lord has not abandoned me*, Naomi thought. Still, she would miss Evelyn terribly.

In December 1973, Naomi announced at the breakfast table, "I've just written Mrs. Conrique a letter. This morning when I was praying, I felt that the Mexican government has just released two more of the children at the orphanage for adoption. I felt that these children are so in need of a family that we should be willing to take them in. . . ."

Everyone stopped what he was doing. Claudia and Patsy responded with looks of surprise, as if to say, "More children? How can we possibly take care of them?" After all, Naomi's salary at the Foundation and as pastor of the small-town congregation was meager indeed.

Rosa swallowed a big bite of pancakes. Then as if speaking for all of the children, she said, "Well, Momma, whatever you do, *don't* come back here with that boy named *Miguel*. He's *muy malo*—very bad—and would give us all trouble." Around the table, four little Mexican heads, including little David's, nodded in agreement.

Naomi felt such an urgent burden on her heart that she actually arrived at the orphanage before her letter reached Mrs. Conrique, now the head of Los Niños. On that quick trip, only her father, Eli, accompanied her.

"Have two of the orphans been released for adoption?" Naomi asked Mrs. Conrique.

"Yes," Mrs. Conrique replied. "A small boy named Roberto Rodriguez and a bigger boy named Miguel."

It turned out that ten-year-old Miguel and seven-year-old Roberto were brothers.

Roberto was a beautiful, soft-spoken child, his expressive eyes, fringed with long lashes, were warm and loving. Miguel, however, was skinny, scowling, and obnoxious to everyone except his little brother. At times Roberto bore the brunt of Miguel's bitter hatred.

Their adoption turned out to be very quick— the Mexican officials processed the papers in only seven days. It was a miraculous answer to prayer! Naomi had urgently wanted Miguel and Roberto to be in Oregon in time for them to experience the joy of a family Christmas.

That Christmas was the happiest in her life— a perfect holiday complete with glistening snow. The new children had never seen snow before and had never had a Christmas tree. They appreciated everything with the total wonder and joy felt only by children who have never known a home and a family.

To the normal celebration, Naomi and Claudia added an enormous piñata. "We can't keep on calling ourselves the Waltons!" Patsy laughed. "From now on we'll be the 'Walton-itros!' " The name stuck.

In the midst of that bustling, noisy household, there was truly "peace on earth." Then the "calm" quickly disappeared.

Take warning, Lady! We want this Center shut down *now*.

The ominous note had accompanied several strange phone calls. They all started in January during the construction of a new house for the growing "Walton-itros."

Why would anyone want to get rid of the Foundation? Naomi wondered. When Tom Higgins, the men's supervisor at the Foundation, expressed his concern, Naomi tried to reassure him.

"Don't tell the others," she told him. "We don't want to worry them. I'm *sure* those are just harmless reactions from some cranky, old person in town who hates long-haired kids. Maybe they're from some kids whose drug pal has been converted and dried out. In any case, don't worry, Tom." Naomi seemed so confident that Tom crumpled up the notes and discarded them.

Then in March, Naomi, Tom, and Claudia were involved in the accident that would leave Naomi in the body brace for many pain-filled months. "Sandy has arrived" would be the next entry in Naomi's diary for March 1974.

PART THREE

Taming the Tiger

CHAPTER ONE

"Sandy, stop it! Help! Someone help me
with Sandy!" Claudia's frantic voice resounded
throughout the house.

A fight was obviously going on downstairs.
The yelling and scuffling caused Naomi to jerk
her head up from the pillow. But the sharp
bolt of pain in her neck, the blood pounding in
her ears, and the whirl of sickening dizziness
reminded her how slowly she still had to move.

By turning on her side and then easing herself
upright in one careful movement, Naomi was
able to stand and walk cautiously down the hall.

Sandy had been in their home for three
days. When he wasn't swallowing his food in
great, eager gulps, he was sitting quietly in the
living room, passively staring out the window
or watching TV with the children. Up to this
point Sandy had caused no trouble at all. *What in*

the world is happening now? Naomi wondered.

Entering the living room, she stared at Sandy in amazement. He sat sullenly on the upholstered couch, his hair and clothes dripping wet. Billy, Robert, and little David stood beside him, their eyes wide and wondering. Manuel stood nearby with a big grin on his face. Claudia was planted firmly in front of the couch, her arms crossed and her blue, Irish eyes blazing. "She took a shower with her *clothes on!*" she said, her voice trembling with anger. "With her *clothes on*, Naomi! Now she's dripping water all over the house! And she's *ruining* the couch. *Do something*, Naomi. I can't *budge* her!"

Naomi did something—she laughed. Manuel laughed. Then Victor, Robert, and David started laughing. Finally, Claudia saw humor in the situation and began to chuckle.

Sandy sat stone faced, but when Naomi gently took hold of his arm, he allowed himself to be led to an uncarpeted bedroom.

"I didn't even *think* about this!" Naomi told Claudia. "Sandy doesn't have a change of clothes and maybe hasn't had one for a long time. She must've gotten used to taking showers in the beach bathrooms of California and just letting herself drip dry. We should've tried to tell her we had plenty of clean clothes for her to change into."

"Oh, Naomi," Claudia repented. "I'm sorry! I keep forgetting the poor kid's had no one to teach her *anything*."

On impulse, Naomi walked to Rosa's closet and pulled out a simple cotton dress. *Maybe*

Sandy would like to dress like a girl for a change, she thought.

That was a bad idea. Sandy savagely tore the dress from Naomi's hands, threw it on the floor, and stomped on it.

Naomi's own eyes glistened in anger, but she controlled it. "Well, she's obviously *not* used to looking like a lady, Claudia. Hand me some jeans and a shirt from Manuel's drawer. They're about the same height. Sandy's used to street clothes."

Naomi and Claudia placed the jeans and flannel shirt in the room with Sandy and motioned for him to change. When they walked out the door, he slammed it and locked it behind them. He stayed in the room for almost an hour. When he came out, he was wearing the clean, dry garments.

"I think she understands now," Naomi told the rest of the family.

But Sandy obviously did *not.* For months, Sandy would continue to shower while fully dressed. Maybe he was nervous about the rickety lock on the bathroom door, afraid that someone might accidentally catch a glimpse of his body while he bathed and know that he wasn't a girl.

"Never knew a street kid to be so doggone modest," Claudia grumbled.

"Maybe it just makes sense to Sandy to wash body and laundry at the same time!" Patsy said, trying to make Claudia and the others smile.

Naomi wasn't sure. In her own mind, she

thought they might simply be dealing with the youngster's iron will—a very strong and determined one at that.

The proper way to take a shower wasn't the only subject on which Sandy and Naomi locked horns that first month. In almost every situation, their "houseguest" was obstinate, angry, and rebellious. *She obviously thinks she is tougher than I am, Lord,* Naomi prayed. *Help me to stay firm. Help me to show her that your strength in my life is greater than even the violent strength of the street gangs.*

Some issues were unimportant to Naomi; some were not. Sandy simply refused to sleep in a bed at night. Naomi gave in on that point. Sandy couldn't seem to get comfortable on a mattress. After all, he'd been used to the hardness of the floor or the ground. His favorite sleeping position was lying across the doorway of the bedroom to which he was assigned.

After a few weeks, Sandy began to sleep stretched out just inside the front door of the home. "Let her be," Naomi wisely decided. "I think what we're dealing with in this case is fear, not rebellion. Maybe she's learned to sleep near doorways so she can make a quick getaway if she has to. Only Jesus and time can deliver her from fear."

Whenever there was a thunderstorm, Sandy would literally "freak out," as the children called it. Although he could no longer hear thunder, he could feel its jolt and see the lightning.

The first time a storm hit the coast that spring, Sandy screamed and raced through the house, breaking dishes and a lamp and kicking over furniture. He opened the front door and dashed out into the pouring rain, running madly across a meadow toward a thickly wooded hillside.

"After her!" Naomi yelled to the oldest children.

Manuel, Rosa, and Miguel galloped across the field after Sandy. They tackled him in a puddle which left them all plastered with mud and dragged him back to the house. Naomi wrapped a big blanket around his trembling body and held him tightly.

"Thank God we don't live where lightning storms are a common occurrence!" Naomi exclaimed when the lightning storm was over.

Sandy needed correction when it came to his "street language," which he could convey in spite of the fact that he could not speak. When Sandy didn't get his way, he threw violent tantrums; the vile gestures he used were easily understood. In those instances, the iron-willed child of stone found himself up against the woman of steel, for Naomi would not tolerate obscenity in any form, spoken or unspoken. Slapping his hands did no good. Naomi eventually discovered that depriving Sandy of part of his supper, such as the homemade pies which often comprised dessert, was an effective discipline tactic.

Taking Sandy to church or involving him in family devotions presented an even more challenging problem. Sandy would hiss and spit whenever he read the name "Jesus" on anyone's lips. Bible pictures elicited great fury.

Even heads bowed in prayer could set Sandy off on a rampage.

"I hate God," he signed to Naomi. "Don't speak about his love. Sandy has no need for Jesus." Many times he stormed out of church in the middle of a service.

His "no need for Jesus" reminded Naomi of the words of the man of Gadara in Luke 8:28. The demons in the man had cried out:

What have I to do with thee, Jesus, thou Son of God most high? I beseech thee, torment me not.

Naomi realized that years of deprivation and abuse had caused Sandy's heart to turn against God so that Sandy would learn of God's love only through the love of God's people. She saw Sandy through eyes which were different from the social workers and state employees who had tried to reach this animallike being. To her, Sandy was more than a troubled soul inside a handicapped body; Sandy possessed an eternal spirit. Naomi knew that areas of Sandy's spirit were as bound as that man in Gadara had been.

Still, at the word of Jesus, that man had been totally freed! Not speaking of it to anyone, Naomi began to pray silently and continually against any evil forces which kept Sandy from being free.

Naomi, Claudia, Patsy, the children, Tom, the workers at the Center, and the men and women of her church—all recognized that the battle to help Sandy had to be fought on different fronts at the same time. He had various needs: food, physical care, instruction in the everyday tasks of living, mental healing from years of drugs and alcohol, acceptance and friendship, love combined with firm discipline, and freedom in his spirit.

Naomi had no "pat answers." While asking God for healing one day at a time, she also relied on him for daily wisdom.

Every time discipline was administered, Naomi knew she faced the possibility that Sandy would run away. And Sandy sometimes did, out of anger. During that first month, he would often disappear for a few hours; once he stayed out overnight.

One Tuesday morning Naomi tried to convince Sandy to go along with her to a doctor for a checkup. Naomi's physician wanted to take more back X-rays, and she knew he would gladly examine Sandy. Sandy's health was a big concern to Naomi. From time to time, the teenager seemed to have some sort of seizure. Naomi wondered about his deafness. Could something be done to restore his sense of hearing?

After patient coercion, Naomi got Sandy into the car. But at the first stoplight, Sandy swung the door open and bolted down the street. He returned home after two days. Naomi decided she'd wait until the iron-willed teenager was *ready* to see a physician.

"Naomi, come and *see this!*" Claudia whispered as she leaned out an upstairs window and gazed toward the front lawn. Naomi joined her and the two quietly laughed together as an amazing scene unfolded in the yard below.

Naomi had given Sandy an assignment that day: "Watch over the two little ones, Robert and David, while they play outside," she had said.

Sandy liked all the "Walton-itro" children. He knew that those kids, like himself, had no "permanent papers." Thus he had an affinity for them. In fact, Sandy no longer let anyone say he was Indian; he'd decided he was Mexican!

Sandy was especially drawn to the two little boys, Robert and David. Because of their age, they were unembarrassed to talk to Sandy in "signs." Besides, they had picked up Sandy's peculiar sign language more quickly than the adults had. After four weeks, the communication among Robert, David, and Sandy had become quite advanced.

Now, Sandy was performing his assignment of "watching the boys." Black hair flowing in the wind, Sandy was marching back and forth like a guard along the curb in front of the yard where Robert and David were playing. His jaw was firmly set; he even carried a switchblade in his right hand.

As the women looked on, a young man from the Foundation came up the sidewalk and attempted to cross the lawn to the front door. Sandy stood directly in his path, held out the switchblade, and made a low, gurgling noise which sounded almost like a growl. It was a comical scene, but Claudia still ran downstairs quickly, motioning that it was OK for the young man to cross the lawn. Sandy submitted. Nevertheless, after that, in case Sandy was "on guard," Naomi's acquaintances phoned ahead before they'd attempt to visit.

Sandy had brought the switchblade with him from Santa Cruz, and the family had never tried to take it from him. He felt he had found his place of importance in the household. After only two months Sandy seemed a permanent part of the Walton-itros.

Often when she prayed, Naomi thought of the violent past symbolized by the ugly knife. *All Sandy knows is violence. How will we ever be able to reach her heart? Did we find Sandy too late, or is there some way that she can change?*

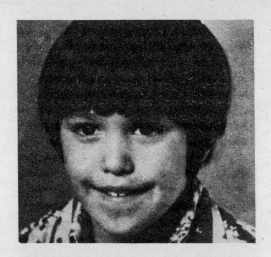

David (top) and Robert (bottom) who
died in the tragic fire at ages six and eight

CHAPTER TWO

No one but Naomi and Tom knew that threat-
ening notes had been sent to the Foundation.
They were also the only ones, besides Claudia,
who knew what Lawyer Rex Boatman had
said about the accident with the semi.

Naomi had first contacted Mr. Boatman in
California when she was still in the hospital
there. She'd felt that she needed a nearby
law office to help handle the medical bills that
would be astronomical. Naomi explained that
the accident had very clearly been the trucker's
fault.

"What kind of work do you do, Ms. Tanner?"
the lawyer had asked.

"Why I'm a pastor and I run a drug rehabilitation center in Hidden Bay."

"That's interesting, Ma'am, because the truck
which sideswiped your van is part of a line
which is under investigation for drug-running

between Mexico and Seattle. Maybe, Ms. Tanner, this 'accident' was planned to scare you or harm you because you know too much. I'm one of the few lawyers around who even know of this investigation because I'm working with the FBI to provide search warrants."

Naomi pondered his words, but she wouldn't live in fear; she was simply too preoccupied to worry.

At midnight on May 16, she heard footsteps on the outside stairway leading to the unfinished upper floor of her home. Claudia, who shared a bedroom with two of the children, also heard loud noises on the wooden stairs. Patsy King, in another bedroom, went to her window to discover a strange car parked outside.

Patsy quickly went to Naomi's room, and the women flipped on several lights. A door slammed and the car sped away.

Who could it have been? A curious teenage prowler? A would-be burglar? "They should know from the looks of this place we have nothing valuable to steal!" Patsy commented. Naomi said nothing.

Patsy phoned the men's dorm at the Center. Tom and several of the men searched the grounds. They found no one, so the women calmly returned to bed.

At 1:00 A.M. two nights later on May 18, Naomi lay awake on her bed, uncomfortable in the back brace. She had just changed the diaper of a two-month-old baby girl who was sharing her bedroom.

Suddenly, Naomi heard a crackling sound.

Thinking that someone had plugged in the artificial electric log in the living room, she got up to check. Naomi opened her bedroom door. The entire hallway was engulfed in flames.

"Fire!" she screamed. "Fire! Everyone wake up! *The house is on fire!*"

She closed her door and raced back to break the window. Clasping the baby in its blankets, she jumped out of the window and ran on the grass to the other side of the house.

Claudia had heard the screams and she and Sandy were already standing on the lawn. After giving Claudia the baby, Naomi ran to the window of the room occupied by Miguel, Billy, and Manuel and broke the glass.

Patsy had awakened Lillia, the young Mexican woman, and helped her get her crippled mother and the three children to the safety of the lawn. Patsy then ran to Naomi's side and helped the three oldest boys climb out of the window.

From the corner of her eye, Naomi saw that nine-year-old Victor and thirteen-year-old Rosa had safely escaped from their room on the other side of the house. They were racing across the field to the men's dorm, screaming, "Tom! Tom! Call the fire trucks!"

By this time only a few moments had elapsed, but the fire was already a mighty inferno. Black smoke billowed from the windows. Fierce tongues of flame could already be seen on the upstairs roof. Naomi instantly calculated that almost everyone was now out of the house— everyone except Robert and David, the two youngest.

"The babies!" she screamed. "Robert and David! Who has seen the babies?"

The panic of fear almost choked her as she ran around the corner to the window of the little boys' room. Using a big rock, she hit the glass. The windowpane exploded outward, driving splinters into her face and arms. In a crazed frenzy she tried to climb into the room, all the time screaming the names of the two boys. She thought she heard one of the little ones call, "Momma!" but the flames and poisonous smoke drove her back.

On the lawn she grabbed a blanket, threw it over her head, and began once more to climb through the window. She struggled with the clumsiness of the back brace. By this time the fire department had arrived. Two strong firemen grabbed her and dragged her away from the house.

"Help me! My two little boys are in that room!" she begged with a raspy voice. She struggled to pull away from the men, but they pinned her to the ground.

"It's too late to go in by that window!" one of them yelled. "It's impossible! We'll try other ways!"

Claudia was trembling as she came to hold onto Naomi. Naomi remembered Sandy had been at her side. Suddenly, Naomi realized she'd heard Sandy say, "Don't worry, Momma! Sandy will get your babies!"

Naomi didn't know *how* she could have heard Sandy speak. Could it be that Sandy's muteness was not physical after all, but psychosomatic, and that the trauma of the fire had shocked Sandy into talking? Or could it be that the Holy Spirit had actually allowed Naomi to "hear" exactly what Sandy was thinking? Weeks later Naomi realized that it was possible that Sandy had actually uttered those words.

In any case, Naomi was *positive* Sandy was now inside the blaze, groping for Robert and David, the two who were so special to Sandy's heart.

"Sandy! Sandy! She's gone back into the house after the babies!" Naomi screamed.

"She couldn't have!" Tom yelled. But a quick check around the yard showed Sandy was nowhere to be found. Tom ran to the living-room end of the house where the firemen were trying to enter.

"The Indian girl—Sandy—we think she's gone back in there!" he shouted.

Sandy had, indeed, reentered the burning building. Standing behind Naomi when she had broken the bedroom window, he had seen fragments of the glass fly ten feet away. Sandy was unafraid, but knew he couldn't enter that way.

The Indian was determined to get to the babies. *Sandy's not important to nobody,* he thought. *So I am the one to go in after the boys. Those babies are important . . . important to Big Momma. They're too little to get out alone.*

Someone had glimpsed a figure dive into Naomi's bedroom window. Quickly several fire-men entered the room and found Sandy crawling beneath the cloud of smoke toward the hallway. It took several grown men to grab his feet and pull him back from the hall. The youth kicked and scratched with every ounce of strength in his body. Just as they yanked him out the window, the entire room was engulfed in flames.

For two hours Naomi sat motionless on the front lawn while Sandy, the children, and friends huddled around her. With glazed eyes, they watched the home burn to the ground.

An ambulance took Victor and Rosa to the hospital. Victor had cuts on his feet and burns on his arms. Rosa was suffering from smoke inhalation. Naomi's physician, Dr. Ben Buchanan, arrived and begged her to go with the ambulance, but she refused to leave until the fire was out. The others insisted on remaining by her side.

The confusion around Naomi was filled with the voices of firemen, policemen, neighbors, and Foundation staff workers. Naomi couldn't hear them. She was in another dimension, separated from the world by a great gulf of horror and heartbreak. She couldn't speak. She couldn't cry and she couldn't pray. In the fiery furnace before her eyes, her babies were dying. She'd never experienced a darkness like the darkness of that night.

Then with crystal clarity, Naomi recalled every detail of the day before. It was Saturday, but she had gone to the Fiesta Café to supervise the varnishing of the new tables, which the men at the Foundation were building. In the middle of her work she had had an irresistible urge to take all of her children on an outing. She hadn't been physically able to do that since before the car accident in March.

It was a rainy day, but she'd decided on a spur-of-the-moment picnic. "Grab all the kids," she phoned Claudia. "Have them help you make a ton of sandwiches, and throw in plenty of cookies and special treats. We're going to the state park for a family picnic. It's been too long since we've done something special together!"

"All right, Boss Momma," Claudia laughed, happy to see Naomi feeling so healthy and excited. "And we'll pack plenty of raincoats and umbrellas. It's a crazy day for a picnic!"

Everyone had had a wonderful time. They'd stuffed themselves in the seclusion of a cozy, covered area while the rain beat a happy rhythm on the roof. Then the sun peeked out, and the children raced for the playground, making sure to jump into every puddle along the way since "Momma" had insisted they wear rubber boots.

"If anyone saw me bringing my kids to the park on a day like today, they'd think I was an awful mother! But look how much fun they're having," Naomi told Claudia. Sandy had signed to them that he had never in his entire life been on a picnic.

When it was time to head home, a muddy, giggling group crammed into the van. The head count was taken: Naomi, Claudia, Rosa, Sandy, Manuel, Miguel, Victor, and Billy were present.

"Where are the two little boys?" Naomi asked.

She trembled involuntarily. Those two were so precious to her.

She rolled down the window of the van. "Robert, David, where are you?"

Sandy pointed to the slide. Yelling "Watch us!" the two tots zoomed down together, head first, and landed with a big splash in the huge puddle at the base of the slide. Everyone in the van roared with laughter. For three years, those little ones had been the joy of the entire household.

Now they're gone. Naomi moaned inwardly.

Finally, while the gutted shell of the house was still smoking, Dr. Buchanan gently led Naomi and the rest of the children to an ambulance destined for Harbour View Hospital.

Naomi was treated for shock, smoke inhalation, and exhaustion. Her back was put into traction until a new brace could be made.

The next day, cards, letters, flowers, and telegrams began arriving. Neighbors and townspeople went by the hospital to offer their help, but Naomi was a broken woman. She didn't want to see anyone.

You're all offering to help now, she thought, but where were you before? Where were you when I was begging for help to start the Foundation so I could help your kids? Why haven't you been to visit and speak encouraging words to the young people who are trying so hard to get out of the pits where they've fallen? Where will you be two weeks from now when I'm still grieving for my two little boys? I know where you'll be. Right back in your attitude of not caring.

In anguish, Naomi turned her head toward the hospital wall. With a sobbing groan which came from deep within, Naomi broke the silence she had entered ever since the fire had taken her two beloved boys. "Oh, *God!*" she cried aloud. "Don't let me get *bitter*." But that morning she didn't believe that even God himself could save her from the tidal wave of bitterness she found bearing down upon her.

Question after question mounted in her mind. They all came together in a pounding refrain: *Why? Why? Why?*

A few minutes later, her sister Nina came to get her checked out and take her home. Nina pushed Naomi to the front desk in a wheelchair. At the desk, Nina stopped to sign Naomi's release form. As they sat by the switchboard, Naomi heard the receptionist answer an incoming phone call. "I don't know, Ma'am," the woman spoke into the receiver. "Let me put you on 'Hold' while I find the answer to your question." She then left the desk to get an answer to the caller's inquiry. The "Hold" button flashed on and on, indicating the caller was waiting for an answer.

As Naomi watched the simple scene, the Holy Spirit spoke to her heart: *Put your questions on "Hold" for now, Naomi. Don't allow those flashing questions to devastate your faith. Just put them on "Hold" and wait for an answer. The answers will come.*

"My mind is like that flashing switchboard," she told her sister as they drove home, "but I *cannot* let go of my faith."

135

It was urgent that she make her decision that very moment. In the next few months, many more questions would be flashing in her heart and mind.

"Home" was once again the old Walton-style farmhouse they had once lived in. Now it was actually in her father's name. Nina drove her to the house and got her settled in, but that same day Naomi urged Claudia to drive her to the site of the fire.

To their surprise, the women found nothing left but a slab of cement. They were told that the local fire department had encouraged the removal of the debris.

Neither Naomi nor any of her co-workers had given them permission, yet only one day after the fire, a bulldozer had come and scraped away all that remained of the building and its contents. Now there was absolutely no way to discover the real cause of the fire.

Naomi discovered that the small local newspaper had reported that the fire had "probably been caused by a small baseboard heater in the living room of the dwelling." Yet Victor said that he had awakened to the sound of fire even before he had heard her warnings. He had escaped by going through the living room area and had actually *stood* on the baseboard heater so he could break the picture window and climb out. The area around the heater had *not* been on fire, even though flames had been overhead.

Naomi was troubled. *I have to know the real cause of the fire,* she thought. Trying to gain some peace of mind, she phoned Hidden Bay's fire marshal, Mr. Holmes, but was disturbed by the man's gruffness. Maybe he just felt defensive about the way he was handling his job. At any rate, the call certainly didn't give her peace of mind. She would have been very disturbed had she known that the heater would not be sent to the state fire office for inspection until *months* later.

The next few days were occupied with the heartbreaking task of preparing for the memorial service of the two little boys, Robert and David. Her friend, Mr. Owen, the head of the Santa Cruz Drug Misuse Prevention Center came to Hidden Bay with his wife, Diane, to perform the simple service. Deeply touched by Naomi's physical and emotional condition, they planned to stay for several weeks to help direct the Harvester Center.

During this time Naomi spoke with the director of the funeral home. He told her, "I feel the sheriff's department and the fire marshal did a *very* poor job of dealing with the boys' remains. In fact, they hardly brought in any remains. It was actually Tom, one of the men on your staff, who searched through the debris of the fire and brought in the remains for the memorial service. I don't think it's fair to a grieving family to see things handled in this manner." The man shook his head. "I think you should file a written complaint."

The director also wrote a formal letter to the Center, airing his feelings. Tom counseled Naomi to file a complaint for the time being.

That unpleasant information pierced Naomi's heart like a knife. On one hand, Naomi knew the two children had eternal life in heaven—glorious, eternal life, complete with glorified bodies which could not suffer. She believed that even the happiest moments in this life are only a shadow of the *real* joys which lie ahead and that her children were now in a spiritual realm from which they would have no desire to return. She often thought of the text of the memorial sermon: *Children are the greatest in the kingdom of God.*

Still, Naomi was *human.* It had been intensely important to her that the burial be handled with dignity. It had been the last earthly thing they could do for the two dear little boys.

Why wasn't it handled better? Why? The flashing lights on ''Hold'' in Naomi's mind had been growing too numerous to count.

A few days later on May 27, Naomi and Claudia made the two-hour drive to Portland to the immigration office. They wanted copies of the children's adoption papers since the originals had been lost in the fire. Naomi also wanted to know whether Mr. Greene had kept the children's passports containing pictures of David at eighteen months and Robert as a toddler. Those would be the only pictures Naomi would have of her lost children.

Mr. Greene, unfortunately, had been transferred to the East Coast. In his place was Jed Provokono, a man of all business and no heart. He refused to give Naomi the passports, stating that they were the property of the Mexican government to which they should be returned since the deceased children had "no permanent authority to remain in the U.S." He even insinuated that Naomi had made up the story of the death of David and Robert in order to obtain their passports illegally.

"But I *gave* the passports to your office in the first place!" Naomi cried. "And if you doubt their deaths in the fire, all you have to do is call the Takilma County coroner. He'll confirm my story."

Naomi left his office upset and with tears streaming down her face. She couldn't believe how callous he seemed. He'd revealed his prejudice against the adoption of Mexican children and had treated her harshly during this time of grief. She felt as if another knife had cut into her heart.

CHAPTER THREE

During the first week of June, Naomi received photostatic copics of the adoption papers for all of her children. Included in the manila envelope was a sober letter telling her to obtain permanent passes for all the "native Mexicans," or else she'd run the risk of having the children deported.

Shocked by the treatment, Naomi phoned the immigration office immediately. She spoke with a secretary who had become her special friend over the last two years. The secretary confided that Mr. Provokono had gotten an anonymous phone call from a man claiming Naomi was an unfit mother for the children. "That call and Mr. Provokono's feelings about 'wetbacks' must be the reasons for his harshness to you," the woman added.

Naomi's head was swimming. *Who would make*

such a call? No one had *ever* accused her of being an unfit mother. More red lights flashed in her mind.

Earlier, she'd written to the county district attorney, requesting that a deeper investigation be made into the cause of the fire. On June 6, she read in the local paper, *The Chronicle,* that the D. A. was investigating the fire "because of complaints from Ms. Tanner and the Harvester Center."

Naomi went to the courthouse to meet the D. A. After introducing herself, she politely asked him, "Has your investigation turned up any other possible cause of the fire?"

"You don't have to introduce yourself. I *know* who you are," he replied curtly, "but I have *nothing* to say to *you.* My report, when it's completed, will go to the sheriff and only the sheriff. I wish you and that newspaper would leave me alone!

"You might as well know that I *don't* like you and your Foundation. And I speak for the sheriff and county officials as well."

Naomi left the courthouse thoroughly confused. Hadn't she lived in Hidden Bay for most of her life and been a respected, law-abiding citizen? She had had no idea that any negative feelings on the part of the authorities existed toward her or her work. Now it seemed as if the quiet, wholesome town she had known was fast becoming scandalously similar to the community in the song, "Harper Valley PTA."

On June 12, Naomi and Claudia drove to

Salem, the state capital, to visit Senator Warren McHardy. The senator had served in the U.S. Senate for twenty-eight years. He proved to be both helpful and understanding, a bright page in what was becoming the darkest chapter of Naomi's life. He offered to get a legal "stay" on the children to prevent their deportation. Also he suggested that Naomi travel to Mexico to obtain from the orphanage certified copies of all the proceedings which had led to her adoption of the orphans.

That evening Naomi, her father, and Claudia sat down at their dining-room table and planned the trip to Mexico. She determined to push aside her uneasiness about both the circumstances of the fire and the cold treatment she had been given ever since the tragedy.

"After all," she told Eli, "I've been through an awful wreck and that horrible fire. I can't let any crazy, unproven suspicions get the best of me."

But even as she spoke, the phone rang at the Harvester office next door. The visiting Mrs. Owen who answered was startled by an ominous male voice: "Whoever you are, tell Naomi Tanner that she is a dead woman." The phone clicked; the line went dead.

Later that night, Naomi answered the phone in her kitchen. "Listen, lady," a male voice said. "I'm sorry about the boys. The fire was not meant for them, but for *you*."

On June 13, a woman phoned the Harvester Thrift Shop and said, "Naomi had better leave town or she's as good as dead." The following day when Naomi was on her way to Ralph's supermarket, a cream-colored Mercedes Benz began to tailgate her car. Two men were in the car; one was talking on a C.B. When Naomi reached the store, the car sped past her, missing her car by inches. Ten minutes later, the phone rang at Naomi's house. Claudia answered it.

"Ms. Tanner is shopping now at Ralph's. Tell her we know where she is at *all* times," a man said. The line clicked. Silence. By the time Naomi returned home, Claudia was crying hysterically.

Another call came on June 16: "Tell your lady boss to keep her mouth shut about all she knows." Naomi was trying to piece things together. *What does he think I know?* she wondered.

The following day Naomi contacted her California lawyer's office to see what progress had been made in her case against the truck company responsible for her back injury. She was informed that Mr. Boatman had been missing for several weeks. His wife and associates had hired private detectives to search for him.

On June 21, Naomi, Claudia, Patsy, and five of the children returned home at 11:00 P.M. from a church service. Suddenly the smell of smoke filled the air. The fire was in their old garage. A large, red couch was in flames and had been pushed under Naomi's father's twelve-foot boat.

Fortunately, they were able to extinguish the fire before it reached a gas tank. Two fires, one on May 16 and now this one on June 21, could not be accidental. The officer who arrived on the scene wrote in his report. *This was obviously not an electrical fire or a case of natural combustion.*

Two days later, Naomi took a twenty-minute drive to visit an investigative attorney, O. R. Benson. She found a parking place directly in front of the four-story office building. While she was telling her story to the attorney, fire sirens began blaring outside, making it difficult for her and Mr. Benson to hear each other.

"We don't know who is causing your problems, Ms. Tanner, but you are obviously in the middle of a very complicated situation, and you must take all of the legal precautions possible," Mr. Benson told her.

"Well, why do the local authorities seem so unhelpful?" Naomi asked.

"Maybe there are underworld connections in the local police. There have been rumors of that for years, you know."

Naomi left Benson's office with the sense that at least someone had listened to her problem and had taken it seriously. As she stepped out of the building, she was stunned and totally unprepared for what she saw. Her car had been set on fire. The entire steering wheel had melted; the inside of the car was gutted beyond repair. That was one "accident" too many.

Naomi and Claudia had tried to keep the children as calm as possible during the days and weeks after the May 16 fire. But now, with the garage fire and the burning of Naomi's car, they were beginning to fall apart emotionally.

During this time, Sandy stood by, watching

things in his own silent way. He sensed the tension running through the household and knew that someone was after "Big Momma." Unfortunately, Naomi didn't have much time to spend with Sandy, although what time she had, she tried to comfort him with the fact that he had done all he could to save Robert and David.

On June 30, Naomi, Claudia, and five of the children headed for Mexico to obtain the special adoption papers Naomi needed. They took their time, enjoying the scenery. In San Diego, Naomi left Claudia and the children at a motel, and Naomi drove south to Tecate.

When Naomi reached Los Niños, Mrs. Conrique embraced her. Together, the two women wept over the loss of Robert and David. The next day they drove to the Mexicali courthouse for legal copies of the adoption papers of Naomi's deceased Mexican children.

At noon two men from the Mexican F.B.I. put them under arrest without giving them a reason! The two women protested, Mrs. Conrique in Spanish and Naomi in English. "Shut up!" in Spanish was the only response they were given. The women were taken to the courthouse jail and then transferred to the jail in Tijuana.

They spent five days in a filthy cell crowded with ten other women, mostly young prostitutes. Bugs infested the sleeping mats, and only a smelly bucket was made available for a toilet. The heat was oppressive to the point of making Naomi nauseated. She worried about

Mrs. Conrique who was advanced in years and not used to such harsh treatment.

The two women might have stayed there longer than five days had Claudia not come to their rescue. Claudia had contacted the secretary general of the province to find out what had happened to Naomi. The ordeal left Naomi's back in bad shape; she was also ill from amebic dysentery contracted in jail. Returning to Hidden Bay, Oregon, seemed like a trip to paradise.

On August 7, Naomi got a letter from Mrs. Conrique, and pieces of the puzzle began fitting together. Mrs. Conrique found out that the Mexican F.B.I. had received phone calls from two people in Washington, identifying themselves as law officers. The two said that Naomi had come to Mexico to take orphans across the border illegally. They also claimed that Naomi had a criminal record in the state of Washington and was under investigation for child abuse and the possible murder of two young Mexican boys named Robert and David.

Naomi was stunned by the false information. Who had made the phone calls which had led to her and Mrs. Conrique's arrest? The whole thing had gotten out of hand, to say the least.

On August 8, at 1:00 A.M., someone fired a rifle several times at Naomi's house. The children woke up screaming. Neighbors heard the shots and called the police. An officer and a newspaper reporter arrived in time to see a car with three men inside speed off, but they were unable to get the license number.

Out of desperation, Naomi pleaded with the police for special protection. "But you *are* getting police coverage," an officer told her. Naomi's father bought her a gun and insisted she keep it in her bedroom.

On August 11 Naomi and Tom Higgins went to a town meeting. The meeting was called after the newspaper reported that "Ms. Tanner" and her family were not receiving proper police protection. The meeting was heartbreaking. A sheriff implied that in Naomi's nervous state, she was imagining the attacks.

On August 13 the tires were slashed on several cars around the Foundation complex. That same evening Miguel went out to the small camper-trailer he was using as a bedroom. A strange man jumped at him from inside and threw a knife at him. Miguel ran toward the house and yelled for help. Sandy ran outside in time to see the stranger head off through the woods. The family took a picture of the knife stuck into the wall of the camper and then called the police to get the knife as evidence.

During the weeks filled with threats and near violence, Naomi's back began feeling worse and worse. On August 15 she went to a hospital to have her back put into traction.

Two days later, her parents came into her room, helped her get dressed, and brought her directly home. Their faces were pale. At home, they told her that Eli had received a call from a man who said, "They've tried to make that lady crazy or at least look crazy, but it hasn't worked, so they're planning to finish her off with drugs or something while she's in the hospital. I felt like she deserved fair warning."

At home Naomi tried to rest as much as possible. One time she woke up from a nap and saw Sandy standing guard at her door. Sandy spent most of his time alone, joining the family only at mealtimes. He still refused to let anyone including Naomi, touch him.

Sandy felt deep concern for Naomi and showed it mainly in his eyes. Ever since the night of the fire when the two boys were lost, he seemed more gentle than before.

One thing that still enraged Sandy, however, was any display of spiritual devotion. He hated to attend church services with the family and spit everytime he saw a Bible. He refused to pray with the family at mealtimes. Naomi felt at a loss, because Sandy had been with the family only since they had been going through their living hell.

On August 23 late at night, two young men grabbed Sandy and put a bag over his head. They tried to pull him into a green car, but Sandy used some of the tricks he had learned in the streets. He probably hurt his attackers more than they hurt him. In any case, he was able to escape and got to the house just as the two men were pulling away. That incident convinced Naomi to take her family and leave the area for a while.

In her diary for that date, Naomi wrote:

This is the last straw. I haven't wanted to turn and run, at least not until I could make some sense out of this mess and find out who caused the death of my babies and who wants to see an end to the [drug] Center. But I don't dare stay here without real police protection. And even if I had that, how could that ensure the safety of my kids?

Naomi made plans to take the family and leave the area in the next week. The Owens from Santa Cruz would come to maintain the Foundation and a pastor from Minnesota would be taking her place at the church. Only those three people, Naomi's parents, and the investigative attorney, Mr. Benson, knew where Naomi, Claudia, and the children would be going.

Finally on September 1, the family left for their secret destination: Phoenix, Arizona. Her father, Eli, drove them in a new car. *Today is Labor Day,* Naomi thought in the car. *Ironic. I feel like an old woman, twice my real age. All the labor of the past seems in vain. I don't feel that I have enough emotional strength now to survive let alone raise a family.*

CHAPTER FOUR

In the warm sunshine of Phoenix, Naomi and
her large family found a soothing balm for
their frantic spirits. The children played outside
each day without fear. Naomi, who had felt
so emotionally and physically drained, soaked
up the healing rays of the sun. They became
an illustration for her of God's presence soothing
the soreness of her heart.

Something else was helping Naomi's healing
process. She was working with her hands—
building kitchen cabinets part-time with Sandy
as her helper.

Her father, Eli, had taught her the basics
of carpentry when she was a child. Now in
Phoenix, the smell of wood being sanded
brought back memories of when life was more
simple. Fitting pieces of lumber together
was a source of comfort at a time when many

pieces of her life seemed so rough and un-connected.

The greatest healing came from working daily with Sandy because he learned things so quickly. Naomi couldn't keep from being excited. Sandy could do almost anything in the shop after he'd been instructed one time. Naomi was amazed at his dexterity. Who could have possibly thought that Sandy was mentally incompetent or unteachable? She realized that he had natural creativity.

They worked together in silence, enjoying the beauty of the wood grain and the colors and smells of the hand-rubbed stains. Sandy still could not show any affection other than an occasional, shy grin. In a few weeks' time, though, Naomi watched him progress from an animal-child into a human being.

Because Sandy had learned to do something well, his confidence soared. When the first payday arrived, he received his very own check. It made him so proud that he strutted around the house with it and made a nuisance of himself. The other children would have popped him in the mouth if they hadn't been certain that Sandy would be the winner in any scuffle!

"I don't think we'll ever need to worry about Sandy running away again," Naomi told Claudia. "He sticks by my side like glue; maybe I'm the only one who ever taught Sandy to do something useful."

Sandy had another reason for living—Naomi didn't know about it at the time: being Naomi's self-appointed bodyguard.

Someone's after Big Momma, Sandy thought over and over. *Big Momma does not know how to fight. But I know how. I will stick by Big Momma.*

In spite of Naomi's certainty that Sandy would not run away, Sandy disappeared only a few days later. The family was frantic. Naomi thought that she had almost forgotten to pray during her depressed condition, but she found herself praying hard for Sandy.

Sandy himself could hardly believe what happened. He'd simply walked away from home on Friday night to "look at the town." The Phoenix suburb was different from the streets Sandy had been used to in California. Many blocks of homes looked identical. Somehow his instinctive sense of direction had failed and he was lost.

On the first night Sandy thought, *Sandy will go home in the morning,* and then curled up on a park bench to sleep through the warm, desert night. Daylight was no help. He walked for miles, growing more and more tired, frustrated, and sunburned. By late afternoon, the day had turned into a scorcher, so he decided to find a shelter. He spied an old hound dog crawling into a dense hedge damp from a garden sprinkler. Sandy did the logical thing for someone used to the rugged outdoors: he crawled in beside the dog and waited for the cool of the evening.

Sandy walked throughout most of that Saturday night. By Sunday morning, hunger pains drove him into a 7-Eleven store. He casually sauntered in and stole a box of doughnuts and a can of soda. No one saw the theft.

He hadn't lost his touch even though he had not stolen anything for almost six months. A small voice in his head said, *Momma would not like this,* but he ignored the voice.

He didn't worry about lunch. Why steal more food than he needed for breakfast when he could just find another store and steal something for the noon meal?

It was now late Sunday morning. Behind the 7-Eleven was a small church which looked a lot like the chapel Naomi and the children had been visiting each Sunday. It was white with a cross on top. *Maybe someone here knows Big Momma,* Sandy reasoned and went inside.

The service was already in progress. The congregation was quite small and most of the people were black. Of course, Sandy could not hear the singing, but he could feel the vibration of the organ through the wooden arm of the pew. And Sandy felt something else—the same feeling he had around "Big Momma." It was the same feeling he had had around Andraé, Marion, Shirley, and all the others at Teen Challenge.

After the meeting Sandy hung around, wondering how to communicate the fact that he was looking for "the Big Momma with no man and many kids." A small number of people had formed a circle in one of the aisles. In a short while, an elderly man walked over to Sandy and held up money. "Here," the man said. "We don't know you, but you look like you could use this."

Sandy hesitated. "Please take it," the man

urged. Sandy read the man's lips as he said, "God loves you, and God wants you to have it."

Sandy took the money. Then because he still couldn't figure a way to ask about "Big Momma," he ran out the door. He was struck by an amazing thought. He had received things from good people before, but he had always thought of those gifts as "from Shirley" or "from Naomi." Now *God* had given him a gift! Sandy's mind boggled.

He clutched the money, walked away, and went to another grocery store where he picked up a carton of milk. Sandy had purchased things with "Big Momma" before, but she had always shown him how much money to pay. This time Sandy thought it best to place all his money beside the milk. He had about twenty dollars in bills and a pile of change.

The checker lady gave him a puzzled smile, took a one-dollar bill, and handed Sandy the change. He stuffed the money back into his pocket and proudly left with the milk. *God gave me this milk!* he thought, his face breaking out into a broad grin.

That afternoon Sandy wandered into a Salvation Army building. He noticed that the place had a thrift shop similar to the one operated by the Harvesters in Washington. *Maybe these people know Big Momma,* he thought.

Sure enough, a smiling woman walked up to Sandy and motioned him to the office. She picked up the telephone and began to talk to someone. Naomi had wisely notified the police and many of the local churches to be on the lookout for someone of Sandy's description. In just a few minutes, "Big Momma" and her gang arrived.

The first thing Sandy did was to show her his money. He conveyed to her that the church people had given it to him "from God."

The following Friday, after a satisfying morning of building cabinets with Sandy, Naomi rested on the deck in the warm sunshine.

Suddenly, clearly, without warning, she heard the Lord whisper to her heart, *Go home.*

I can't! she thought. *I can't go back to the hostility of some of the townspeople! I can't go back to the loneliness of seeing the places which hold memories of little David and Robert! I can't go back to the danger!*

But the Voice was persistent like the bright noonday sun: *Go home, Naomi. It's time to go home.*

CHAPTER FIVE

APRIL 1975–APRIL 1976

"Where's Sandy?" Naomi asked. Then she
knew where. Ever since they'd returned home
from Arizona, Sandy and the other children had
often gone to the gravesides of David and
Robert, the two little boys lost in the fire.

The children expressed their grief by frequent
visits to the Memorial Gardens cemetery.
They usually left presents beside the tombstones.
Once, Eli had given Victor a small Tonka
truck which Naomi later found at the cemetery.
That forlorn toy became a pathetic symbol
of the loneliness which plagued the children. Her
adopted children had known Robert and David
in Tecate long before they had become "family"
in Oregon.

Sandy often stationed himself at the graveyard
as if he were still standing guard over the
two boys. "Our babies are not there," Naomi

would insist over and over again. "Their bodies returned to the dust, but their spirits are safe with Jesus in heaven." Nevertheless, the pilgrimages to the cemetery continued.

"Leave them alone," Eli advised. "You all have to have time."

If only their valley of grief could be traveled through quickly! And my battle against depression and despair be won in a month or even a year! Naomi thought.

Naomi found herself praying for strength and wisdom on a daily basis. How else could she sustain the pain and tragedy in her life? Her blueprint for survival was based on two principles the Lord had shown her before she'd left Arizona: *Face your fears; forgive and forget.*

Naomi had concrete reasons for all her fears. She and her co-workers had been in very real, totally unimagined danger.

Yet as she returned home to face all that she was afraid of, those reasons seemed to dissolve. Each time she turned to face a part of her terror, it vanished like a phantom.

Naomi had never known for certain *who* had been after her. Had the drug runners and members of organized crime thought that she had inside information on their activities? Had some of the town's policemen and elected officials been "bought off" by the mob? Surely no small-town hoodlums could have blown up her car or had her run off the freeway in California or had her thrown into jail in Mexico! Perhaps some of the phone threats and bizarre events had come from that element of kooks who hear about a situation and complicate it by heartless pranks.

And why hadn't there been more support from the authorities and townspeople who *were* honest? Were they so set in their small-town ways that they simply bungled the investigation? Perhaps they had accepted the view that "the preacher lady was just imagining things" so that their city could remain comfortably free of scandal.

Naomi sensed that it had been a combination of all those factors which had nearly destroyed her. And more than any person masterminding the entire, complicated scheme was Naomi's diabolical spiritual enemy.

Why haven't I recognized this before? she pondered. *I've even stood in the pulpit and taught the truths in the book of Ephesians:*

> For we wrestle not against flesh and blood,
> but against spiritual forces. . . .

I carried the gun that my father gave me. I went to the courts and to the lawyers. I was only wrestling against flesh and blood. I must learn to do some spiritual wrestling as well. From now on, I have to use the spiritual weapon of prayer more and more.

When Naomi returned to Hidden Bay, she had fully expected more threats and more rejection from the local townspeople. The threats never came.

The Taco Fiesta Café and the thrift shop had been closed down. Though the Harvester Foundation was still helping many drug addicts, it was not a "live-in" situation. Perhaps the new lower profile made criminals view the Center as less of a problem.

Something else had also happened during Naomi's absence. Several local law officers had been dismissed for corrupt dealings in other situations. Whatever criminal element had been influencing the county seemed to be losing its power. Now the complaints Naomi had registered seemed much more valid in the eyes of her community.

In addition to her fear of violence, Naomi's fear of rejection also turned into a phantom. In fact, there were apologies, not rebuffs. Naomi was often approached in the shopping mall or the post office by individuals who said, "We're so sorry about the fire, about your children, about all the ridiculous things said about you in the paper and at that town meeting. We're glad you've come home."

Naomi had also dreaded possible rejection by her church family. She had somehow sensed that many of the church members were embarrassed by the stir which had engulfed her as their pastor. The interim minister who had been called in was a man. Naomi perceived that some in the fellowship felt that the church would be better off "without a lady in the pulpit."

However, in her absence, Naomi's flock had realized what a gifted teacher and preacher she was. Upon returning, they flooded her with the love and respect due any gifted leader, male or female. When the interim pastor left, Naomi's reinstatement was unanimous.

Another fear which dissolved as she faced it was the situation at the immigration office and the conflict over the legality of her children's visas. A new director with the understanding of Mr. Greene, her friend of the past, had recently taken charge of that department. The new man had received excellent reports on Naomi from the social workers who had known her for years. He saw that the Mexican orphans were finally issued permanent citizenship papers.

Naomi had learned to face her fears. The next step would be harder. She had determined to make someone "pay" for the fire which was, in reality, the murder of her two little boys. She had tried to force the law to track down the killer or killers. Yet no amount of effort could undo the past and set things right.

For weeks, she struggled with the realization that there could be no getting even. *Why, I can't even identify the ones I'm trying to get even with!* she thought.

Forgive and forget. It is the only way you and your family will ever overcome the grief. The words came back to her.

But how can I forget, even if I forgive? she thought. Then she read one verse of Scripture which became a foundation stone for her:

Will not the Judge of the Earth do right? . . .

"More than ever I'm seeing that God Almighty is on a different timetable from us," she shared with Claudia. "His schedule is *eternal*. In eternity, the Judge of the earth will make everything just and fair. I have to leave judgment in his hands. It isn't easy for me. I want to fix things on my own, but the Bible has so much to say about not taking vengeance into our own hands. The Judge of the earth will do right in behalf of Robert and David."

Daily struggles continued, but little by little, Naomi found she was climbing out of the pit of emotional destruction which she knew Satan had dug for her.

The following Friday morning, Naomi and Claudia got a frantic phone call from a young woman named Rachel Williams. Rachel had been converted at Harvester's, but then she had met and married a violent drug addict named Paul. Rachel was young and deeply troubled. Not capable of being a good mother in her present condition, she had nevertheless had two babies.

"Come get these kids!" Rachel sobbed into the telephone. Both the infant and the toddler were screaming in the background. "Their crying is driving me insane, and I know I can't cope any longer. Someone must get here right away!"

Naomi and Claudia arrived at Rachel's tiny, cluttered apartment within fifteen minutes. Filthy and terrified, two-year-old Israel was crouched in a corner. Six-week-old Eli was in even worse condition. His skin was covered with sores; he looked as if he were starving to death.

Both women wept over the little ones as the took them home. They tried to convince Rachel to go with them. She refused to leave Paul, even though he often beat her and had sometimes beaten young Israel.

That week the County Foster Care Services told Naomi that Rachel had legally assigned the boys to the foster care system. "Since she knows you're licensed for foster care," the social worker told Naomi, "the natural mother has requested that you keep Eli and Israel and raise them as your foster children."

"No!" Naomi declared. "No, I can't! I can't take those two babies into my heart and begin to raise them as my foster children, knowing that the system could rip them away from me in the future. I can't face the loss of more children after Robert and David."

"Will you keep them for a while, Ms. Tanner?" the social worker pleaded. "Just until they're healthy?"

"Yes," conceded Naomi. "I'll keep them for a while."

Tiny Eli was suffering from malnutrition and required almost constant care. He could take only a few ounces of formula at once. By feeding him many times a day, by speaking to him gently, and by cuddling him continually, Naomi nursed him to health.

As Naomi talked to her tiny charge, she had a hard time calling him "Eli." "He just doesn't look like an Eli!" she told Claudia. "I wonder what his middle name is."

Claudia phoned the foster care office and

asked the social worker for Eli's middle name. "Naomi, Eli's middle name is *Robert!*"

Within the month, Naomi heard once again from the social worker handling the Williams' file.

"Ms. Tanner, I've heard from Rachel again," the woman reported. "She has signed permanent relinquishment papers for her two children and has requested that we offer you the opportunity to *adopt* them."

Naomi protested, saying, "I'm not ready for this. Besides, I've tried to adopt children in this county before. As a single woman, I've found I'm just not eligible. And I don't think my home is big enough or my salary adequate for me to gain approval for more children. . . ."

" . . . Well, shall I send our caseworker to do a home study and see?" the social worker replied.

The caseworker arrived the next day, much to Naomi's surprise. It usually took months to get a home study done.

The caseworker was rude, gruff, blunt, and unsmiling. She seemed to look upon the entire "Walton-itro" household with disgust. She did everything except openly accuse Naomi of being a lesbian with the wrong motives for wanting to adopt.

Somehow, miraculously drawing on the new inner strength she had gained in the past months, Naomi did not lose her temper. Sandy sat near "Big Momma" during the entire interview, his eyes wide with perception. As soon as the woman went out the front door,

Sandy exploded with obscene gestures. The social worker's manner infuriated him. "I am OK," Naomi signed. "This is what I thought would happen."

The following week Naomi got a certified letter, requesting that she appear in court with her lawyer and the children "regarding the pending adoptions" on April 15.

In the courtroom several days later, Naomi stood in a daze before Judge William Wright, the same judge who had granted permanent papers to Manuel, Miguel, Victor, and Rosa. He greeted her warmly.

"Ms. Tanner, this court sees fit to place Eli Robert Williams and Israel Williams in your care."

"You mean that I can adopt these children?" Naomi was stunned.

"*Are* adopting, Ma'am. You will, I assume, be willing to handle the usual legal costs of this adoption?"

"Oh, yes, Your Honor. Yes, of course!"

"And you are prepared to assume the financial responsibility which will be yours in their upbringing?"

"Yes, sir, I am. But what about the home-study report?"

"The home study?"

"Judge Wright, I'm positive that the home study which the State did was not in my favor. In fact, the interview went so badly that the caseworker must hate me."

"Not in your favor!" the judge exclaimed. "Why, Naomi, that home study was *100 percent favorable*. The caseworker was so impressed by your character, even when she *tried* to make you angry, that she finished her report by stating that she would gladly be adopted into your home!"

Naomi was speechless for one of the few times in her life.

"And how are the little ones doing?" the judge inquired.

"Pre—pretty well," Naomi managed to stammer. "At least little baby Robert is doing well. Israel is still terrified and shakes like a leaf every time we even say his name. Apparently about the only time his parents called him was when they were about to strike him. We have to whisper his name when we talk about him to each other; even hearing us whisper 'Israel' makes him run and hide."

"We're changing his last name today," the man observed. "Maybe you should choose a new first name for him, too. If his mind associates the name *Israel* with abuse, why call him that any longer?"

It was a very sensible suggestion. Before Naomi could even answer, the Judge continued. "Let's see. Israel. Perhaps his mother gave him that name for a reason," he mused. "Well, David was the great king of Israel. You could perhaps call the little boy 'David.'"

That suggestion had to be of God. It was so clearly the work of the omnipotent Lord, for the judge had known neither that Naomi's two youngest children had died nor that they had been named Robert and David. Judge

Wright had no idea he was a part of God's plan of restoration for Naomi's life.

Once again the arms of the entire Tanner household opened wide—this time to embrace two precious little Caucasian boys, unbelievably named Robert and David.

TOP: Carpentry skills help give Sandy self-esteem

BOTTOM: A more contented Sandy

CHAPTER SIX

"Momma, I am ready," Sandy signed.

"Ready?" Naomi was puzzled. Sandy had marched into the living room from the front yard where he had been performing his duty of guarding the newly adopted toddler named David.

"Ready?" Claudia was also puzzled. "We aren't going anywhere today, Sandy."

"Sandy is ready," the youth repeated. Then he bowed his head and folded his hands as if to pray.

"Sandy is ready," he conveyed for the third time. "Sandy is ready to talk to Jesus." The teenager dropped to his knees.

After all of the altar calls Naomi had given in services where Sandy was present, after all of the meals when they had attempted to get Sandy to bow his head, after all of the times he had shown a heart of stone, Naomi could hardly believe what was happening. Sandy was actually kneeling, "ready" to ask Jesus into his heart!

Naomi and Claudia fell to their knees and prayed out loud for Sandy. Naomi was in tears.

"Do you know that Jesus is really here with you, Sandy?" she asked when they finished praying.

Yes! Sandy nodded. Then he grinned his crooked grin, tossed the long hair out of his eyes, pulled his switchblade out of his pocket, and marched back outside to the front yard to continue guarding.

The two women, like sisters for so many years, looked at each other and began to laugh. "We should have known!" they told each other. "We should have known that when Sandy finally received Jesus, it would happen just this way!"

Sandy had actually felt Christ's presence in his heart during that moment of commitment. But Sandy remembered that that was not the first time he had sensed God's love.

He had sensed God's love years before in the lives of Shirley, Marion, Mom Hall, and all the other dedicated staff at Teen Challenge.

He had heard God's love when he listened to Andraé Crouch put that love into song.

He had seen God's love when he first met "Big Momma" and had responded to it by signing, "My eyes will see you again."

He had been touched by God's love through the hands of Claudia as she had fed him, through the church members who had hugged him, and through friends who had accepted him as he was.

He had received God's love even at the hands of total strangers, such as the little congregation in Phoenix which had given him an offering and conveyed that it was a gift from the heavenly Father.

No, this was not the first time that Sandy realized that God was with him. But now all of the prayers offered in his behalf and all of the attempts made to break through a heart of stone had somehow merged in one moment to bring Sandy to salvation.

That day when Sandy knelt to receive Jesus, Naomi attributed it to the miracle of God's restoration in the form of the two brothers named Robert and David. That miracle had deeply touched Sandy, yet even that restoration had not been the catalyst for the stone boy's conversion.

The reason for Sandy's total commitment to the Lord Jesus Christ is best told in his own words, which he conveyed in sign language:

Many, many times people have wanted to know what finally made Sandy change. I thought and thought about the answer for many days and it finally comes back to one main thing: people giving me their time, Big Momma giving me her time.

This boy Sandy is very hard-headed. Sandy always acted like he felt nothing for nobody, like my insides were a rock. But Momma gave me her time and was a friend to me. I saw her in all those hard times, and that preacher is the strongest person I ever saw.

To me, being adopted is everything. There are a lot of little people [children] out there in those foster homes and on the streets that want to be adopted. Before Naomi, people tried to buy Sandy some papers [legal adoption], but Sandy had messed up bad in the early days and finally people gave up on him. Sandy was not one thing good or bad to anybody. But Sandy messed up at Big Momma's, and she still gave Sandy more time.

It took much time for me to see a need in my heart. Then, in Oregon came the night of the big fire. I tried to help the preacher lady get our little boys out, but I could not get those babies.

That was the blackest night and a night of many tears.

A long time after that, Momma woke up in the night, screaming for Robert and David to come to the window. I saw her looking so lost for many, many days. But then she decided to go back to the Jesus house and start preaching again.

I did not understand this, but Naomi told me that Jesus could take all of this bad and somehow turn it around. I would not believe her, but I thought, This preacher momma has guts.

Time went by and she was getting stronger like steel. Now Sandy is one mean boy, but this momma is tougher than Sandy.

She spoke to me that this strongness was because Jesus was helping her to be strong. Deep inside, Sandy knows this is right—I see that I need one many times stronger over me.

Sandy is hard-headed, but finally came the

172

day I was watching the new Robert and David. After much time with Momma, I decided I was ready. So Sandy went in right and told them.

I said, "Sandy is ready for Jesus."

PART FOUR

Sorting out the Pieces

A now peaceful, happy Sandy with his horse
named "Sandy"

CHAPTER ONE

MARCH 1977

"Is this Naomi Tanner?" a man's voice asked gruffly.

"Yes. Who is this, please?"

"A federal investigator. My name isn't important at this time. I have been asked to locate a person named Sandy, and I have reason to believe you may know where I can find the child."

Naomi's heart raced. She bit her lip and struggled silently for calmness and strength.

"Ms. Tanner, do you know the location of a young person named *Sandy?*"

"I know a teenaged girl named Sandy," Naomi answered slowly. "She has lived in my home off and on for several years. But I'm afraid I can't help you because Sandy isn't here now. In fact, I don't know where Sandy is."

That wasn't a lie. According to a simple note, Sandy had left home several days before to visit friends. Naomi knew Sandy would return, but at the moment of the investigator's call, she honestly didn't know Sandy's location.

"Does this young person who has been in your home appear to be of Indian or Mexican descent?" he asked.

"Well, . . . perhaps," Naomi murmured.

"Is this Sandy about four-foot-eleven, thin and small boned, with waist-length black hair?"

"Well, yes, sir. . . ."

"And is Sandy deaf and dumb, totally unable to communicate?"

"Sort of. . . ."

"*Sort of!* Come on, Ms. Tanner!"

"She communicates with *me!*" The stranger's rudeness turned Naomi's fear into anger. "She communicates with the boys and girls I have adopted. She communicates with our neighbors. She. . . ."

"Ma'am, listen to me!" he interrupted. "I believe this is the Sandy I'm looking for. The trail led me all the way from Los Angeles right to your doorstep. All of the pieces fit. Sandy was last seen here in Oregon. But you keep referring to Sandy as 'she.' It may be a great shock to you, Ms. Tanner, but if this is the kid I'm looking for, then Sandy is a young *man.*"

The investigator stopped talking long enough to give his words a chance to sink in.

Was Naomi shocked or even surprised?

Once, she would have been very shocked. But after months of dealing with this teenager called Sandy, absolutely nothing about this complicated personality could come as much of

a surprise—not even the revelation that
this young girl whom she loved so deeply might,
in fact, be a young boy.

Pieces of the puzzle which made up Sandy's
incredible story suddenly snapped into place.
"Yes, sir, that could be," Naomi said, breaking
the long silence. "Sandy has never let me or
any of the children into the room when she's
been changing clothes. When we've tried to get
her to a doctor, she's run away and hidden
out for days. In fact, for the first year of Sandy's
association with us, she took showers with all
her clothes on."

"Her clothes *on?*"

"Yes, sir. Sandy has no whiskers and doesn't
need to shave like a teenaged boy should,
but this child has been through so much that
there are probably hormonal problems."

"Yet you say that Sandy *communicates* with
you?" The man sounded remote and unbe-
lieving.

"Oh, yes! It took a long while—a very long
while, but now we communicate. She—he—has
his own sort of sign language and reads lips very
well. We all understand each other perfectly
around here. Sandy is even learning to read
now, and has become quite a carpenter. She
helps me a lot in the business I own."

Now it was the inspector's turn to pause in
silence.

"Then there must be some mistake. This may
not be the missing person I've been tracing," he
mused after a lengthy pause. "The file I have in
front of me right now tells the story of a little boy

who became a ward of the state of California when he was approximately six years old. He was severely mentally, physically, and emotionally handicapped and was finally labeled 'totally unreachable.' One of the state's social workers had such a time with him that he wrote in his report: *Extreme deprivation has produced what can only be labeled as human garbage!"*

Naomi shivered. How could anyone have called her Sandy "human garbage?"

"The child was so violent and harmful that he had to be institutionalized," the voice continued. "After escaping from various children's homes, he was finally committed to the state mental wards and is scheduled for re-evaluation only when he reaches the age of twenty-one."

"Why are *you* searching for Sandy?" Naomi finally asked.

"Ms. Tanner, Sandy is *still* a ward of the state of California. He has no other legal guardian. It seems, however, that he has somehow managed to escape from every mental hospital in which he was confined. At this time, one of those state institutions is under federal investigation. The institution is still receiving money for Sandy, and for others like him, who haven't been there in *years*. That is why Sandy's case has surfaced after all this time."

"What will you do if you find him? Will you take him back to California with you?" Naomi's voice trembled.

"I've been asked to bring Sandy back if I can," the investigator stated without feeling.

"Would he be recommitted?"

"That's a possibility. It's not up to me, Ms. Tanner. As I said, Sandy has no legal guardian, not even a last name, and he is still a minor."

No! Not now! Naomi thought. *Not after all we've been through together! Not after all the progress Sandy's made! Not when Sandy has finally received Jesus as Savior.* Naomi decided to sound not like a mother, but like a lawyer with some authority in her voice. She began to plead Sandy's case.

"No one from Sandy's past could even recognize him," Naomi said. "The changes in him are nothing short of miraculous. You *can't* take him back! You just *can't.* How can you bind him to these reports of the past? Sir, please give him a chance." Her voice finally broke. "He's had so few chances."

The investigator struggled as he listened to the story. Should he respond according to what was best for this child or according to his duty as a federal investigator? The hellish boy in these reports must have required superhuman love and dedication. The woman had told him that it had taken her a year to teach the child to sleep in a bed! How could anyone send him back to the horror of a state mental hospital? For the first time in years, the inspector pushed aside his sense of duty.

"Ms. Tanner, if you do happen to see Sandy in the future," he said, certain that she would, "give him this advice. Tell him it would be unwise to return to California, even for a visit. Tell him there are warrants out for his arrest all over the state."

"What are *you* going to do?"

"For now, nothing. If even half of what you say is true, these changes are *miraculous*. I think I will just keep this file in my possession for a while. But you must be aware of something, Ms. Tanner. Besides this federal investigation, Sandy has the problem of a police record a mile long. I may not be the one to take him in, but probably someday somebody will. Good night, Ma'am."

The line clicked. Silence. Naomi hung up the receiver and slowly slumped down onto the family's old, weatherbeaten sofa.

Naomi didn't cry. Her expressive golden brown eyes, oblivious to the homey surroundings, stared into the growing shadows of evening. They saw only a kaleidoscope of memories from the last five years.

The conversation had left Naomi so numb that she hadn't even gone to turn on the lights as darkness filled the room. She sat motionless for an hour, returning to the present only at the sound of the front door opening and closing.

From the sound of the footsteps, Naomi knew Sandy had returned home. He entered the living room, grinning and tossing his head so that his thick, black mane swung away from his eyes. Then he saw Momma, sitting alone in the dark. Something was desperately wrong.

He walked to her side. His eyes met her eyes, and then he began to read her lips.

"Sandy," she was saying. "Once and for all, you *must* tell me about your past. And this time, you must tell me *everything*. Start with the very earliest things you can remember."

CHAPTER TWO

EARLY CHILDHOOD

How does one piece together memories? Early
childhood memories are often hazy and im-
complete. A typical adult remembers a pet, a
favorite toy, a room he had at three or four years
of age. For Sandy, the fog of memories as
a very young child is even more dense, due in
part to the confusion of the years that followed.
Sandy signed the following story as best he
can remember it:

*The land was flat with very few trees and no moun-
tains. There was a home or shelter of sorts, but
from early morning until late at night, the little boy
sat outside. He felt very hot. Sitting on the ground
in the scorching sun, he cried for a drink of water.
The winds stung his face with desert sand. Other
times he was extremely cold. The sky and the earth
looked gray. On those days he cried because he was
shivering.*

*There were big people, several of them, but no
mother, no father. The big people had to leave each
morning. The little boy was tied to a long rope
outside in the yard. He had dirt to dig in, rocks to
play with, but nothing else. Sometimes there was
a dog for him to watch—sometimes two or three. The
boy never knew where the big people went nor why
he couldn't go with them.*

*In cold weather, sheep also occupied the yard.
The boy loved the sheep. When he was cold, he could
lie between them and feel warm and sheltered
from the icy wind. Years later, sheep would be the
only things to bring a smile.*

*There were wildly crashing thunderstorms on
the prairie. They would leave him petrified. Massive
purple clouds would roll across the plains, collide
over his head, and explode with streaks of lightning.
The sheep and the little boy huddled together,
drenched by the rains and shaken by the thunder.*
Perhaps the sky is angry with me, *the boy thought.*
He would bury his head and cover his ears.

*[The fear of storms would eventually become
so deeply rooted that even as a teenager, the boy
would run for cover and dive under a bed to avoid
the brightness of flashing lightning.]*

*At least once, a storm grew so severe that lightning
jumped from the sky to the ground nearby. Time
after time, blinding streaks bombed the ground near
the boy. A tree or a bush would be hit. Then the
crackle of fire and the smell of smoke would be added
to the nightmare. The dogs and the sheep could
run away, but not the boy. He was tied. All he could
do was scream.*

[How did the fire end? Did it burn itself out,

or did the big people come home and put it out?]
*Perhaps one of the big people, someone important
to the boy, was lost in one of the fires. But the boy isn't
sure. The details are lost. Only the terror of the
fire remains.*

*One day the big people took the boy and left the
plains. There was a big yellow bus for making
journeys with many big people friends and little
people friends.*

[To whom did the boy belong?]

*No one special looked after this child. He feels that
he just belonged to the group which belonged to the
bus.*

[Where did the bus go?]

To a place with many trees.

*One time he lay down for a nap in a big box under
one of those trees. An angry man found him,
kicked him, and yelled at him for being in the box.
The boy ran to the bus for safety, but he was too
small to climb up the steep stairs. He crawled under
the bus and cried.*

*There were many days of travel on the bus. Finally,
the group went to work in a field of trees near
a town. One day, some of the bigger children walked
into the town, and the boy followed. There were
many buildings and many cars, and someone gave
him some candy.*

*The big people must have worked near this town for
several months. Perhaps they were in the Southern
California orange groves. The streets of the town
became more and more familiar to the little people
who were too young to help the big people with
the harvest.*

The little people found wonderful parks and playgrounds. When they were hungry, they mooched food or stole it or sometimes picked through garbage cans outside restaurants. As small as he was, the boy learned his way around. His instincts developed quickly. He always knew exactly where he was. Sometimes he would even leave the other little people and find his way home alone after dark.

[Did anyone in the group warn him about coming in alone or discipline him for being so late?]

No one seemed to notice.

[How did the boy come to be separated from the big people, totally on his own? Did the group leave him?]

No, they did not leave him. They continued to work in the same groves for a long time. One day the boy just left them.

The bus was parked in a place where the big people started working. The boy would run up and down through rows of trees with other little people.

He was used to being on his own and was so familiar with the city streets that he felt at home there. He probably never decided to run away from the group. Perhaps he would return someday, but he never did.

And that is how the little brown-skinned boy who was so alone on the prairie became even more alone in the city. He was only four or five years old at the time.

CHAPTER THREE

After conveying his memories of early childhood
via his now well-developed sign language,
Sandy sat with Naomi in the living room and
shared with her everything he could remember
of his entire past. That past is, of course, recorded
in the first few chapters of this book.

As Sandy shared the events which had taken
place at the mental institution, Naomi clearly
saw why Sandy had allowed everyone to view
him as a girl. No wonder he showered with all
his clothes on and had refused to be examined
by any doctors during his life on the run.

"Momma," Sandy signed. "Do you love
Sandy as a boy as much as you did when you
thought Sandy was a girl?"

"Oh, Sandy!" Naomi cried, catching him
up in a bear hug. Tears filled her eyes. "Girl
child or boy child, it makes no difference
to your family. We just love *Sandy*."

For some time after the new revelations about Sandy, Naomi and her adopted family lived in fear that the federal investigator would call again and that Sandy would be ripped from their home and institutionalized in California. Then in 1978, Naomi was finally able to convince Sandy to see a physician. The medical report stated that Sandy was at least twenty-one and therefore no longer a minor in the state of California. The circuit judge of the city of Hidden Bay declared Sandy a resident of the state of Oregon.

In 1979 Sandy and Naomi and Mari Hanes, the author, were able to travel to California together to substantiate Sandy's story through eyewitness accounts, police records, and institutional reports.

In the months since Sandy's open commitment to Christ and his return to an identity as a male, great progress has been made in his life. No ability to talk has been recovered thus far, however. As stated earlier in the book, his vocal cords are badly damaged. He is still restrained verbally, probably due to deep-seated, subconscious fear. Sandy's doctor feels that on the night of the terrible fire, Sandy, gripped by the trauma of the situation, actually broke through that subconscious barrier and spoke the words, "Don't worry, Momma! Sandy will get your babies!" So, Naomi probably had not just imagined Sandy's words.

With an increasingly refined medical technology, it is possible that Sandy's hearing may someday be partially restored. At the present time, however, Sandy communicates beautifully with his sign language and by the radiance on his face. The "wild child" has grown into a uniquely gifted and special young man.

Sandy often shares his testimony (with an interpreter from the family) in churches and youth groups. People of all ages love and accept him immediately. When he walks into a room, everyone senses that this once tormented being is a great reservoir of peace and love. It is amazing to watch the way toddlers and children flock to Sandy. Perhaps that is because they sense his compassion, love, and gentle manner and are thus eager to sit on his lap.

Sandy is still growing and feels that he has so much to learn and relearn. He shared the following information. It pinpoints where he is today in his continuing spiritual and emotional development:

Sandy is learning to do many things. I now feel very good about eating at the big table with other people and do not feel embarrassed. I now know how to act at most times.

I have a motorcycle bike and can go on all the trails and dirt roads around our house. I also have a horse and this year I got to ride it in a parade.

Sometimes I still don't understand what people tell me. This Thanksgiving I saw Momma [Naomi] say she was going to dress the turkey. So, to be of much help, I took the turkey to the bathtub and gave it a nice bubble bath. [Sandy had, of course thought that Naomi meant she was going to put clothes on the turkey.] *I forgot to tell this to Momma, and she couldn't find the turkey until she walked into the bathroom and discovered it in the tub.*

How everyone laughed! Now when people laugh about things I do like that, I laugh too and don't get mad because they love me.

You see, I, Sandy, want everybody to know that there is no wild person inside my head anymore. The wild person had to go out when Jesus came in.

Sandy says, "The
wild person had to go
out when Jesus came in."